Y'ALL EAT YET?

Welcome to

THE PRETTY B*TCHIN' KITCHEN

MIRANDA LAMBERT

WITH HOLLY GLEASON

WE GONNA GET A BIG OL' SAUSAGE
A BIG OL' PLATE OF RANCH-STYLE BEANS
I COULD EAT THE HEART OF TEXAS
WE GONNA NEED SOME BRAND-NEW JEANS

—GUY CLARK, "TEXAS COOKIN'"

CONTENTS

Nonny with the Thanksgiving turkey

INTRODUCTION

I never thought I'd be writing an introduction to a book like this . . .

If you know me or my music, then you know I love and live life on the fly. It's about having fun and being in the moment. And part of that is my amazing friends, making memories, people feeling welcome, and mixing up a crazy good time everywhere we go.

I never thought about how lucky I am. Looking back on all these recipes and the memories they contain, I shake my head. I was raised by two generations of women who know how to whip up a party, a home-cooked meal, or enough light bites to feed an army, the way most people roll by the drive-through window.

That was never the way with this band of gypsies, down-home hell-raisers, and hardworking women who knew how to make people feel good. To us, it was a matter of what's in the pantry, how do you pack it, who's bringing what—and what else do we need?

From the time I was a little girl, there were always people around. My nonny had a bunch of girlfriends, and they'd get together at the end of the day to catch up, laugh about what had gone on, and have snacks and drinks before they went home to put dinner on the table.

Nonny was the original Ya-Ya, like in Rebecca Wells's book *Divine Secrets of the Ya-Ya Sisterhood*. Nobody did a holiday feast like she did! And she was very stubborn about *how* she wanted it. She taught me the value of traditions, of using food as a way to punctuate the day and give people a sense that they were cared for.

To this day, people talk about Nonny's cookies—and her Thanksgiving dressing. She'd say the secret "was in the hands," but I think it was in the heart. Everything she cooked, you could taste the love.

As glamorous as they came in East Texas, Wanda Coker had a knack. For delicious. For bringing people together. For having a good time. For jacking that hair up, making people stop and smile.

She passed that knack on to my mama, Beverly. I've never seen *anyone* do more with less! Out of an almost-empty pantry, she could make a dinner that would be fit for a king, Dolly Parton, or the preacher. And it wouldn't be a meal of making do; it would be something so delicious people would talk about that time they dropped by Bev Lambert's and she fixed up whatever concoction she'd come up with.

Me, Mom, and her '80s hairdo

My brother, Luke, and me helping Mom in the garden

That was the thing about my mom. Before people were thinking about nutrition, organic food, or balanced diets, she was doing it. We grew our own vegetables and raised chickens and rabbits. She wasn't a hippie who'd gone back to the land but a working woman determined to put the best possible food on her family's table.

And it wasn't just about feeding us either. People from all over knew if they were in trouble, they could come to us. We'd have ladies and their children arriving in the middle of the night, staying with us while getting their lives figured out.

My mom also never met a stranger. It's just a matter of how long until you actually met. She loves people like no one I know. You'll be fast friends from the moment you strike up a conversation with Beverly Lambert. But not all friends are equal. Some are lifers.

L to R: Heidi, Vicki, and Mom

She and my dad made deep friends when I was growing up. Denise, Heidi, Vicki—whom you'll meet shortly—were Mom's soul friends. Each showed me ways of looking at the world that still influence my songwriting; they also showed me different ways to make people feel loved.

When I started thinking about all the ways these women came together—often with me up in the mix, from the time I was small—I realized how much a little bit of something to snack on figured into all of it. Whether it was a potluck, a cupcake tower, some salsa, or a homegrown stir-fry, some of the truest conversations happened over chopping, setting out, or just reaching for one more bit of something.

And when my dad was around, there was a pretty good chance some songs would break out. My dad, whose band played my tenth birthday party, is also a pretty good cook. He's in here, too, teaching you the right way to season cast iron, a few campfire recipes, and other hijinks.

But really, this is a book about friendship across the generations; about the way food brings, binds, holds you together; about laughter, tears, true confessions, celebrating, and even coming into your own.

Too many people worry about Instagram perfection, about making something so complicated or exotic that everyone goes *"oooooh."* That ain't us. We'd rather laugh, crack a beer, and tell you where the plates are! Load up, sit down, and enjoy the moment. It's supposed to be easy, supposed to be sweet. Even when we've gone to some effort—and a few of these recipes take real work—perfection's the last thing we want anyone to worry about.

So here, from my family's pretty Bitchin' Kitchen—where you can laugh 'til your sides hurt, share what's got you down, or cheer your latest victory—to yours. Pull up a chair, get something cold, and let's take the pressure off!

Nothing says "We're glad you're here" more than a little sumpin' you've thrown together. Open this book, laugh along with three generations of true Texas women, and create your own Bitchin' Kitchen, a place where your friends can come, hang, and savor the time without worrying about anything at all.

Denise and Mom

Dad and his guitar. Where do you think I got it from?

1

WHO'S IN THE BITCHIN' KITCHEN?

▼▼▼▼▼▼▼▼▼▼▼▼▼▼▼▼▼▼▼▼▼▼▼▼▼▼▼▼▼▼▼

If you're going to have a Bitchin' Kitchen, you're going to need a lot of high spirits and friends who, like you, can get a job done. Not everyone needs to have the same strengths or tastes, but together you come through every single time.

Growing up in Texas, watching my mom and her friends, I saw the way pitching in, working together, loving music, and being there for each other are the greatest gifts you can have in life. I think *my* mom inherited that gift from *her* mom, because they both attracted the most awesome groups of girlfriends. All these women would come together, cut up, sometimes dress up, and share everything life could possibly hand them. And 99 percent of the time, they were together in the kitchen making deviled eggs and chili, drinking whatever struck their fancy, and talking about whatever the local news, secrets, hopes, and the song on the radio might be.

I watched female bonding up close and personal from a very young age. I can close my eyes and see the slow cookers all lined up on the counter as news got passed around. Those smells and whatever the news might've been mingle even now, taking me right back to everybody in the kitchen chopping, mixing, stirring, and sorting out life.

When I talk about my mom's tight group, her ride-or-die, be-there-always girlfriends, the ones we call the Ya-Yas, I mean Denise, Heidi, and Vicki. Those four have been through *everything* together: sickness, health, crisis, triumph, death, birth, boys, men, dogs, cats, and a whole lot of music. Whatever it is, they're all in—and they have a damn good time doing it.

Watching them, together and on their own, taught me a lot about how to get through life, who to lean on, how to find a smile when it's tough going. Friends, food, laughter, celebrating the good and the bad with people you love—it's pretty simple stuff, but it's also everything. Life is going to happen, and it's up to us to decide what we're going to do. Even more importantly, it's our decision how we're going to feel about it!

To me, food doesn't solve your problems. It really doesn't change anything. But when it brings the folks you love closer together, it's a good glue for those moments that need holding together. The longer I live and the more I travel, the more I realize how lucky I am to have grown up this way. I always thought other young women were also surrounded by strong, opinionated women they could count on and experience life with.

We're not the fanciest (though every one of these ladies can set a table!) or the bougiest, but we are absolutely, unequivocally the funnest. When we get together there's no stopping us from having a big time. So from our Bitchin' Kitchen to yours, here's to the easiest way we know of making memories to last a lifetime.

Now, before we begin, let me introduce you to this cast of characters— or rather, this band of fierce hearts. I know you're going to love them as much as I do.

NONNY (MY MOM'S MOM AND MY GRANDMOTHER)

"Do what you can with what you got."

Nonny. Mom's mom, my grandma, and a true force of nature. There are so many things I think of when I think about Nonny, starting with food, love, and entertaining. She would make the most basic things, things you didn't think were special—and when she made them, you couldn't get enough.

She had a big goose cookie jar, and after school we'd run over to this ceramic bird and take his head off. Whether it was filled with Pecan Sandies or her famous homemade Nonny Cookies, we'd grab handfuls. Those Nonny Cookies, as we all called them, were the classic chocolate chip cookies that every mom and Girl Scout made. So did my nonny, only when she baked them, they were something else. To this day, people still ask after those cookies like they were the greatest cookies ever made.

Not that Nonny bought into any of that. She acted like her cookies were no big deal. When you'd ask her outright how she did it, she'd look at you like you were crazy, then say, "Well, I use the Toll House recipe right off the chocolate chip bag. I don't do anything special." She swore she didn't. If you pressed, she'd hold up her hands with the fingers spread out, bring them together then open them back up a few times, saying, "It's all in the hands." To this day, we haven't figured it out, and we've all tried.

It was that way with so many things she'd cook. She took all her secrets to the grave, which was just like her! She knew the power of sparkle and the power of intrigue. She was Dallas stunning when we were little, just the kind of lady who made people's heads turn. And when she moved down to Lindale to be closer to us, she didn't slow down her own special brand of glam one little bit.

Nonny had her own crew of friends. They'd all gather up on her patio at the end of the day. They'd come together, compare notes, have a few cocktails, laugh, and then get home to put dinner on the table. That power of strong women's friendships was such a source of joy, strength, support, and just enough "trouble" to make life interesting. My mom learned from the best of the best.

My high-low thing started with Nonny too. She'd put deviled eggs on a crystal platter, but use paper plates for her guests to make cleanup easy. She would have us all to dinner with the good china, but she and Pop-Pop would eat in the kitchen at her island.

She loved traditions, holidays, family, friends, and being together. To her, those were the things that mattered. She was incredibly generous with her love, and with her sense of wherever we were, it was absolutely the place to be—she passed that on to all of us too.

BEVERLY JUNE HUGHES LAMBERT (BEV)

"Be who you are and stick with it!"

Bev is my mom. We like to say Mom is a cheerleader, who shows up for everyone and believes in everything they do. She was born a true Texas girl who started cheering while she was in junior high. She went on to become the head cheerleader in high school, in a state where that really matters, then a varsity cheerleader in college, where cheerleading is practically treated as a religion. Spunky, brunette, and pretty, she was all sparkle. Obviously, she could get everybody riled up! I think it is fair to say the people who know her would say she *is* a cheerleader in every sense of the word.

But her biggest and best cheerleading has always been for my brother, Luke, and me, since the moment we were born. Whatever we wanted to do or fell in love with—horses, dogs, singing, cooking—she was right there, encouraging us, showing up, and making us feel like we'd already succeeded.

And I can truly say that Luke and I are both living the *exact* lives we wanted, in part because of how Mom cheered us on. What a gift.

She taught us both a lot about cooking, how what happens in the kitchen is a good way to understand how to create all kinds of things we want in life. It doesn't matter what you don't have—figure out what there is and get cookin'!

That's how deep the idea of using what you got and making something really yummy runs in our family. My mom's specialty is one of the greatest lessons she taught me. She can literally use whatever she has in the house and make something delicious out of nothing.

Many times, I've seen her go into an empty cupboard, drawer, or refrigerator and create something wonderful with a can of tomatoes, an onion, and something fresh from the garden, adding some oregano and letting it simmer. It wasn't fancy, but you could taste the time that went into it—and the love.

We ate a lot of spaghetti growing up. You can feed a lot of people for not a lot of money with spaghetti, and everybody's happy and full when they're done. With the garden and all those fresh tomatoes, you wouldn't believe how much sauce my mother put up once they started getting ripe.

Mom taught Luke and me this lesson. No matter where I go or what happens in my life, the idea of "use what you've got," no matter what it is, has sustained me. Not just through moments of hunger either, but also through fear, uncertainty, and everything that happens in a life.

DENISE (NEICY) WATSON

"What can I say to help ya?"

I've known Neicy since I was in diapers. A fiery redheaded hippie mama, she's a mom of three and now a grandma to two wild and wonderful grandbabies who have her spark and curiosity. They raise chickens and bees, then jar and sell the honey from their hives. Nobody has more fun, more live-out-loud joy in their hearts than Neicy. She's one of the reasons I love music so much. She always had the best taste, knew all the best artists and music, and could talk for hours about John Prine, Guy Clark, and Jack Ingram. I soaked it all in.

Even more than appreciating the artists, though, Neicy has an amazing appreciation for songwriting. She'll pick out a line, then say, "Did you *hear* that?" Or she'll talk about the way a melody moves, how it picks up the emotion in the song. She taught me to listen for those things. We bonded over music more than I ever realized when I was growing up. You know, when you're young, it is an incredible feeling when an adult talks to you like you're on their level. Even though I didn't realize how much faith she was putting in my taste, I knew I loved talking about music with her more than anybody. She talked about it in a way nobody else did, which gave me a deeper sense of listening and thinking about the songs.

My mom always talks about the first time she and Neicy met. She was my dad's best friend Rod's new wife, which sets up the possibility for a whole lot of everything. But when Mom met her—all 110 pounds with a headful of brown-reddish curls, wearing a pair of overalls—she just fell in love. She laughs about it now, but she went from being loyal to Rod's first wife to not having one speck of "hell, no" for Neicy. She was just so cute and so good inside and out.

Denise is just that kind of person. You can't *not* love her, because she loves everyone and everything so much. She fell right in with our family; she and Rod and her kids literally became part of our tribe. It was like two families blending into one. When I was growing up, if there was something my parents couldn't do, Denise and Rod were there, and my mom and dad would do the same thing for their kids.

Neicy's family is from Louisiana, so one thing she brought with her is the spice. She loves it hot! Hot! HOT! Her Cajun influence on the things we ate was right on time. She could whip up a blackened anything or jambalaya without missing a beat of whatever song she was singing along to. We'd just be there watching, knowing something fiery and delicious was about to hit our tongues.

Over the years, Neicy, whose favorite flower is a daisy, has never missed a single show I've played in Texas. Like her beloved flowers growing alongside the road, she'll follow whatever highway or back road she needs to and find where we are, always bringing those good spirits and a special, spicy treat with her. Neicy loves the road, so sometimes I think coming to see one of our shows is just an excuse for her to merge driving, music, and loving on all of us into one feel-good escape. And it's always awesome when she arrives.

VICKI PLAXCO (PRINCESS V)

"I add strawberries to my cocktails. Just trying to keep it healthy!"
"It's all about the ambiance."

Princess V is our glam girl. Every squad's gotta have someone who knows how to sparkle, to shine, and to kick things up a notch. A true character, the Princess is Texas regal and can quote Princess Diana at the perfect moment. No matter what or who the party is celebrating, Princess V is going to roll in shining, with a perfectly themed dish and all her Tiffany bling blinging bright. She *loves* life, so any excuse to get together and have a party sounds good to her. For Vicki, no reason at all is as good a reason as any to share some snacks, drinks, and laughs.

She's also a professional glamper, a dog mom of two, and a lover of all things Airstream—so it might surprise you to know that she has had a long career in Texas state government.

That's how Vicki met my family. She is a certified fraud examiner. When I was younger, she was the Deputy Inspector General, Enforcement Division, Texas Health and Human Services, and later the Public Manager. But to us, she's the one who's going to bring the fancy and the perfect whatever—and we're not gonna hate her for it.

I think my love of sparkly things, be it guitars, cowgirl suits, or night skies when the stars are out, comes straight from the Princess! She unabashedly loves all these things for what they are, not for what they tell people. Once you've seen someone shine like that, you've got a star to steer by. That's Vicki.

HEIDI PRATHER (QUAHEIDA, PRONOUNCED: QWUA-HI-DA)

"I'll just stop at Buc-ee's on the way down. Do y'all need anything?"

In every group there's that one absolutely bright, sweet ray of sunshine. For us, it is, and always has been, Heidi. She works harder than anyone else I know: she's a wife, a stepmom to two girls, and a rescue dog mom to Ruger, a very high-energy beagle who can't get, or give, enough love. Whatever anyone needs, she knows almost before they do, and she's ready to provide.

Buc-ee's, for example, is our absolute must-go, "Oh my goodness, can you believe they have that?!" *favorite* truck stop. They're all over Texas. And you know when you see the little beaver mascot that you're going to be able to load up on dry goods, a bakery filled with kolaches, a jerky counter loaded with different flavors and meats, a barbecue bar, and too much other good stuff. And Heidi *understands*! That's why her battle cry always includes "What do you need?" when she's on her way; she knows there's always a Buc-ee's between where she is and where we're meeting.

She's a Mary Kay rep, and she knows how to use those cosmetics like a ninja fairy godmother. If you want someone to help you get your glam on, Heidi's the one. She understands how to bring out your best features, just like she knows how to slip a drink into your hand before you even realize you're thirsty.

When I was growing up and we'd head to Austin, it meant seeing Heidi—and what could be better? I've known Heidi and "Princess Vicki," the Fischer sisters, since I was seven or eight years old. They were born and raised in Austin and will always be the essence of that city to me. They grew up where *Austin City Limits* came from. And they, like everyone in our world, *loved* music. When I started chasing my dream, just a girl trying to play shows in bars I was still too young to drink in, they let me sleep on their couch what seemed like a million times.

Literally, they let me sing for my supper. And when you're trying to get something going in the music business, that's a blessing. You get so many feelings thrown at you from strangers; coming home to Heidi and Vicki's house was always a soft landing. And when you're faced with how much bad food is out there on the road—truck-stop "specials"; ugly, flat meat deli trays backstage; late-night fast food—you starve for some home cooking. Anywhere near Austin, I always knew I had a home on the road. And when I got there, Heidi and her sister Vicki always did me right.

Plus, I got to watch their lives unfold. Promotions, weddings, retirements, all life's ebbs and flows—I saw them happen. Along the way I even sang in both of their weddings. Those are the moments when you realize how intertwined life and love and friendship really can be.

ME (RAN)

"It'll all come out in the wash."

I write and sing songs. I'm a stepmom and a dog, horse, goat, and cat mom. My family has a store in Texas called The Pink Pistol, from where we also run our Red 55 Winery, and my husband is from New York. And then there's MuttNation Foundation, my dog rescue organization, to take care of as many fur babies as we can. It's all a little bit of heaven, but the good stuff truly comes together when we all get together.

There's something about having a group of us together—whether it's me with Mom and her friends the Ya-Yas, my band and crew, my girlfriends, or my fellow songwriters—that feels right. "The more, the merrier" is a cliché for a reason: it's true.

To be completely honest, I love eating way more than cooking, but I'm always trying to get better in the kitchen. Like my "aunts," I love what happens when you put people together with good food, drinks, and a fire, on a porch or next to an Airstream. Even a concrete parking lot can be a great place to get together, share some snacks, and play some music if you've got some lights strung up, chairs and tables set up, and mason jars to put flowers in. It's not about the fancy, it's about the fellowship—anything in a pinch, or a load-out.

That's the beauty of the way I was raised: I don't care where I am. I just wanna make people feel welcome, loved, and seen for their awesome. Those are the lessons I learned from my nonny, my mom, and her squad. They were passed on to me and all my friends—and now, with this book, hopefully to you and all your friends and family, who make you richer than all the money in the world.

cheese ball
1 pkg. Cream cheese
1 cup cheddar cheese
(shredded)
1 pkg. Hidden Valley
ranch dressing
mix (pour in as is
mix up +
roll in chopped
pecans

tuna salad 2 cans tuna
(I use only
Chicken of the
sea) in water
drain water out
pour in bowl
& mix ½ cup
sweet pickle
relish, ½ small
onion (chopped)
½ apple chopped
(boiled egg optional)
1 teaspoon sugar
+ 1 lg. tablespoon
mayo or more

2

THE ORIGINAL QUEEN OF THE BITCHIN' KITCHEN, NONNY

▼▼▼▼▼▼▼▼▼▼▼▼▼▼▼▼▼▼▼▼▼▼▼▼▼▼

My grandma was a bombshell, just like a movie star—which is a weird way to talk about your grandmother. But my nonny, Wanda Louise Bass Coker, just was. She had shiny black hair, and she wore it in the biggest beehive hairdo—all these curls, stacked on each other. It looked like this great big, beautiful wedding cake.

With her huge brown eyes, often with the perfect cat's-eye liner, she stood out. She looked just like Priscilla Presley—well, *if* Priscilla Beaulieu Presley was from Texas. They had the same great big eyes and great big beehive hairdo. You couldn't help looking. People did everywhere she went.

She was voted Most Beautiful in her high school *two years* in a row, junior *and* senior years! In Texas, a single year being named Most Beautiful is the biggest deal ever. Two years? Well, that just doesn't happen. It doesn't. But it did.

That was Nonny.

Crazy, magical things happened to and around her. She was a femme fatale, but she really wasn't ever about the drama as much as living her life on her terms. It just so happened her terms were pretty specific and very awesome. If we're being honest, she was a little bit Elizabeth Taylor *and* a little bit Sophia Loren.

My mom says Nonny was so beautiful, she never really had to do anything for herself. Everybody just wanted to do it for her. *I* know she never filled up her gas tank ever, not even once, because my pop-pop always did it for her. It made him happy to do those kinds of little things for her, which is about the sweetest thing in the world.

Even with all of that, the prettiest thing about my grandmother was how much she loved fun, friends, and being together. It runs deep in our veins, that idea of gathering your tribe, loving your girls, making every moment special in some way. You might get a deviled egg on a crystal plate, something that seems a little out-of-the-way kind of fancy, but it wasn't about being fancy at all. That crystal plate was all about telling you how special you are—and how happy she was to be with you.

It was the greatest example of just enjoying the things that make you happy! Don't save it or wait; don't worry about it being what someone tells you it should be. That attitude was the most amazing gift, just watching how she saw and did life. That sense set me on the path of high-low, mix-and-match, put it together and don't worry about everything always having to be the best. That's the path I've been on since I started having a life that was my own. I thank her for that.

Use what you got, of course, but never be afraid to use the good stuff either. Get down the good china or the crystal just because. Just. Because.

I was eight when Nonny moved to Lindale to be closer to us. Before she moved those ninety miles east from Dallas, going to visit her and my granddad was like going to Disneyland. It would be a few days of the most fun and being spoiled with all the good snacks. It's funny how even a bologna sandwich is special when you're eating it and laughing with your grandmother.

But once she got to our hometown, it was even better. Suddenly, we saw her almost every day. It was like we had *two* homes, each so very different in so many little ways. For instance, my mom didn't believe in sodas—or Cokes, as we called every kind of soft drink—and Nonny always had them in her refrigerator. There was nothing like running out of school at the end of the day and seeing her parked there in her white Cadillac with the tan roof. She was so glamorous! Obviously, I knew her as my grandma, but she was also one of those ladies who always had her nails painted. She'd have her nail polish and a sequin cigarette pouch that she'd let me play with. Or some days, she'd let me have a cigarette just to hold, just to hang out the window to feel all grown-up and glamorous like her.

I think I got my love of glitter from Nonny. She knew how to put it all together. I see pictures of her in her little outfits from the '70s and '80s, bright green shorts and a matching top, western shirts with fringe and her cowgirl hat just so. She'd be wearing all kinds of costume jewelry, just looking so fabulous I can't help but smile. She loved all that stuff! And to this day, when I see fringe I am drawn right in. I can't help myself; it's the Nonny in me.

On the days Nonny would come get us after school, it was always an adventure. Some days she'd take us to Dairy Queen to get a Blizzard, or she'd take us to her house and let Luke and me rummage through her refrigerator as soon as we came inside. She didn't want us "prowling," as she used to call it, but she knew we needed our snacks.

Nonny and Pop-Pop's was a little brick ranch house, with three bedrooms and two baths. They had a patio out back for smoking and barbecuing, and they did plenty of both. All the flower beds were full of colors: zinnias, impatiens, azaleas, hydrangeas, caladiums, hibiscus, and tons of roses. Nonny had the most perfectly green yard. I could never get over how perfect it was, with all the grass, the elephant ears with great big leaves, and ferns everywhere. She even had a giant sycamore tree with big, long branches that swept down to the ground.

When I was thirteen, my mom took my first publicity pictures there in that yard, right there by that sycamore tree. If I was going to be a singer, I knew I should plant my feet firmly in that place and take the pictures to send out with my bookings. My grandparents' place felt like a refuge. From the moment you pulled in, it felt—and looked—like the happiest place on earth.

My grandparents had the greenest thumbs, which I was in awe of. They could grow anything, but I can kill a fern. I can kill a succulent. And I did. When I was trying to figure out what to plant at my farm, I called Nonny. I knew she'd have the answer for me. We laughed and laughed. But Nonny knew me. She knew how much I loved the way her house looked. She told me to get azaleas. I did.

I can still see Nonny in her yellow kitchen, that '70s kind of yellow that falls somewhere just short of gold. It was kind of French country, with a border just under the ceiling. And being Nonny, all her appliances and the Formica counters were in this same shade of not quite gold but more than yellow. She had a double door, with a small island.

At Nonny's house, so many of the best dishes were about cooking slow and low—humble food that took time but really paid off in flavor. Red beans were so much a part of who we were, and nobody made them like Nonny! I remember watching her with a can of Coke, pouring half of it into the beans "to stop the farts," then drinking the other half. I figured it must've been the fizziness, so when I started making my own baked or red beans, I decided to use half a can of beer and drink the rest. All these years later, it still seems to have worked out okay.

My grandparents had a whole dining room, with a sideboard full of pretty china, crystal, and the decanters they collected. That was the fancy stuff. They had it all in the dining room, looking so perfect. It showed me the beauty of a lovely table in a lovely room. Pop-Pop would still eat at the island in the kitchen, standing up. That taught me that maybe it doesn't matter where you eat but who you're with.

The prettiest thing about my grandmother was how much she loved having fun and bringing her friends together. That's what she passed down to my mom and me. Nonny liked to make those moments special. Even if it was nothing special, she'd add a special touch. Never to be fancy; just enjoying the pretty things that make you happy.

Her attitude was "Don't save those fancy plates or wait for a special occasion; don't worry about it being what someone tells you it should be." She would mix and match, use high and low, serve on crystal platters and paper plates. She knew it was going to be perfect no matter what. That attitude was 100 percent my nonny, and it's the most amazing gift she gave me.

Nonny and her girlfriends, who I think of as the original Ya-Yas, would be out back on the patio most days, all sitting together, smoking, and having a cocktail. Nonny was very social. She'd be on the phone with all her friends catching up, then right around 4:30 or 5, everyone would converge on her house—having put their dinner in the oven or on the stove—to compare notes.

This was the "original girl gang." Mom has her crew, but Nonny's group! Mom learned from the best—and it's amazing the power of listening to women who're more than sisters talking about nothing, or the latest gossip, or losing a loved one. Whether laughing, shaking their heads, or reaching to give somebody a hug, their collective strength made me feel like your girlfriends are the ones who always get you through.

Nonny's group, though, wasn't playing! When you talk about women who're kickin' ass and takin' names, those were Nonny's girls. Joanne, Pat, Faye, Kay, and Pat's sister Peggy made up this great crew that would descend each afternoon to dissect the day. Each lady had her specific place in the world. Joanne made fancy drapes. Pat was the head charge nurse at the men's prison. Aunt Faye was a school principal in West Texas; after she retired, she moved to Las Vegas and became a principal there, then retired *again*. Kay owned the antique store, which had the most amazing stuff; she usually knew the whole story to go with every item. Peggy, the county commissioner's wife, always dressed up real fancy.

For all that smokin' 'n' sippin', Nonny brought her A game. Nobody made a cheese ball like she did—the grated cheddar, the cream cheese, the packet of ranch, all mixed up and rolled in pecans, served with Ritz crackers. And she'd set it out on pretty crystal.

For how fancy Nonny was, she never stopped being small town too. Breakfast was cheese toast—literally, toasted bread with a Kraft Single— and black coffee. She'd make the best goulash, which was glorified Hamburger Helper, but made from scratch with egg noodles, chunks of roast, mushrooms, sour cream, and paprika. It was just this creamy deliciousness that seemed to get better the second day.

Her lasagna was also a big deal. I remember having it at her house or hearing that Nonny and Pop-Pop were coming over with a lasagna in a big tin pan. We'd just wait for it. It was something so simple, but beyond the cheese and the sauce and the noodles, there was the love. And I swear you could taste it.

REALLY, THOUGH, NONNY'S BIG MOMENT WAS HOLIDAYS. SHE *LOVED* THE holidays. She could go as fancy as she wanted. She liked everything very traditional, and we had to do the same thing year after year. My mom hated it because, with Thanksgiving being so close to Christmas, it was a lot of work, twice, for the exact same meal. Turkey, ham, mac 'n' cheese, Rick's Magic Beans (page 57), and Nonny's dressing. *Her dressing!* Cornbread and celery and onions, broth, the giblet gravy, and a pinch of sage. I can still hear her saying, "Just a pinch, or it'll turn green." It is absolutely the very best stuff you'll ever eat. We're all addicted to Nonny's stuffing—and none of us could ever figure it out.

Finally, this year we *nailed* it! Mom, Luke, and I worked our very collective best magic . . . and we got it. Because my brother Luke's a vegetarian, we also figured out how to do a second version without anything from an animal included. It seems impossible, doesn't it? Somehow, we did it.

Everything Nonny made was just delicious. Her food was simple but nourishing. She'd have on her pretty nugget jewelry or her clip-on earrings, looking so put together while working in the kitchen, ready to feed whoever was there. It made you feel like the snack or meal Nonny was making was planned especially for you, that her pretty table was set to say "welcome," just to invite people to kick off their shoes and settle in.

It's simple stuff you won't be able to get enough of. I know I've been spoiled with Nonny's cooking my whole life. Now you can have some of that same love on your plate too!

Nonny's TUNA SALAD

SERVES 6 TO 8

4 (5-ounce) cans of tuna packed in water (not oil)

3 celery sticks, chopped

1 apple, chopped

1 cup chopped red onion

2 hard-boiled large eggs, chopped

3 tablespoons sweet pickle relish

¾ cup mayonnaise

Spicy mustard (optional)

1 teaspoon kosher salt

½ teaspoon freshly ground black pepper

DRAIN the tuna. Transfer to a medium bowl and break up with a fork. Add the celery, apple, onion, eggs, and pickle relish and toss. Add the mayonnaise and mustard to taste, if using, and season with the salt and pepper. Stir to combine.

COVER and refrigerate the tuna salad for about an hour, then enjoy. It's always good with party crackers, celery sticks, or in a good old-fashioned tuna sandwich.

Nonny's
BLACK-EYED PEAS
OR RED BEANS

SERVES 6 TO 8

1 pound dried black-eyed peas or red beans, rinsed and picked over

1 (12-ounce) package salt pork

1 teaspoon Creole seasoning (I like Tony Chachere's)

½ can (6 ounces) cola (Nonny always used Coca-Cola)

Rice and French bread, for serving

PUT the beans in a bowl, add enough water to cover by 2 to 3 inches, and let soak overnight.

DRAIN and rinse the beans and transfer to a pot. Add enough water to cover by 2 to 3 inches, then add the salt pork. Bring to a boil over high heat, then reduce the heat to low and cook, partially covered, for 2 to 3½ hours. Thirty minutes before serving, stir in the Creole seasoning and cola. Serve with rice and French bread.

Nonny's
BANANA PUDDING
SERVES 6 TO 8

1 (4.6-ounce) box vanilla pudding mix (I like Jell-O Cook & Serve Vanilla)

3 cups whole milk

1 (11-ounce) box Nilla Wafers, a few crushed up and reserved for serving

3 ripe bananas, sliced

1 (8-ounce) tub whipped topping, thawed if frozen (I like Cool Whip)

PREPARE the pudding mix with the milk according to the package directions and let cool. Layer the bottom of a 9 x 13-inch casserole with half of the whole cookies, then top with half of the sliced bananas. Pour half of the pudding evenly over the cookies and bananas. Repeat the layering with the remaining whole cookies, sliced bananas, and pudding. Top with the whipped topping and reserved crushed-up cookies. Refrigerate until cold before serving.

Best
LEMON MERINGUE PIE EVER

SERVES 6 TO 8

MERINGUE

4 large egg whites

¼ teaspoon cream of tartar

Pinch salt

6 tablespoons sugar

FILLING

1 cup sugar

3 tablespoons cornstarch

2 tablespoons all-purpose flour

¼ teaspoon salt

1½ cups water

2 lemons, zested, plus ½ cup fresh lemon juice

2 tablespoons unsalted butter

4 large egg yolks, beaten

1 prebaked 9-inch piecrust

PREHEAT the oven to 350°F.

MAKE the meringue: In a large glass or metal bowl, using an electric mixer, whip the egg whites until foamy. Add the cream of tartar and salt. Beat on medium-high speed until soft peaks form. With the mixer on, gradually add the sugar, a couple tablespoons at a time, until fully incorporated. Continue beating until glossy, stiff peaks form. Set the meringue aside while you make the filling.

MAKE the filling: In a medium saucepan, whisk together the sugar, cornstarch, flour, and salt. Stir in the water, lemon zest, and lemon juice. Cook over medium heat, stirring frequently, until the mixture comes to a boil. Stir in the butter.

PLACE the egg yolks in a small bowl and gradually whisk in ½ cup of the hot sugar mixture. Whisk the egg yolk mixture into the remaining sugar mixture in the pot. Bring to a boil and let cook, continuing to stir, until thick, about 6 minutes. Remove from the heat.

ASSEMBLE and serve the meringue: Pour the filling into the piecrust. Spread the meringue over the filling, sealing at the edge of the crust. Bake for 10 to 12 minutes, until the filling is set and the meringue is browned. Cool for 1 hour, then refrigerate for 4 hours before slicing and serving.

3

MAMA'S MAGIC
▼▼▼▼▼▼▼▼▼▼▼▼▼▼▼▼▼▼▼▼▼▼▼▼
Working with What You Got

Some people's mothers are hilarious. Some people's mothers are crafty. Some people's mothers can get the job done, *whatever* the job is. Some people's mothers know exactly what you need—sometimes even before you do. Some people's mothers can bust butt and take no shit but somehow still seem like the nicest people in the world.

Beverly Lambert—or Bev, as absolutely everyone calls her—is actually all of those mothers rolled up in one. *And* she never breaks a sweat, makes a face, or even has to really try. In a world where women face all kinds of expectations, my mom always laughs and just goes on about being Bev.

It was an amazing way to grow up: to see a woman just be. Whether she was working side by side with my dad doing some kind of stakeout or surveillance job, making cookies for our classroom, creating a real home out of our ramshackle house, growing vegetables, or setting a pretty table, she always looked beautiful, *and* she made it seem easy.

When you're raised around that kind of "can-do," you actually come to believe there's nothing you can't do. That attitude pretty much defines my mom. Well, that, her love of a good time, and her tight group of girlfriends. You have to understand that my mom makes friends wherever she goes. She can talk to anyone, anywhere, and she does; she makes friends with people from all walks of life, levels of education, jobs, hobbies, whatever. We all joke about "the circles of Beverly," because it seems like everyone everywhere who's ever met her is "a friend."

My mom may cast a wide net, with friends all over the place, but she knows that the ones she can always count on are those Ya-Yas. Denise, Heidi, and Vicki are there for each other no matter what.

Watching them—together and on their own—taught me the power of having women friends to lean on. It's pretty simple stuff. But it's also everything. Life is going to happen. Mom and her crew believed it's up to us to decide what we're going to do. Even more empowering, we decide how we're going to feel about it.

One of my mother's greatest gifts is her ability to turn even a tough moment inside out and somehow make it a positive one. No matter what happens or what goes wrong, she is always there for others, finding the good and making something special.

When things were tough for our family, it wasn't a problem as much as it was an absolute adventure. Mom saw to it that we were always looking forward to the next fun thing, whether it was a project we were going to tackle or a dish she was making from whatever happened to be on hand. When she'd start whipping things together, we thought it was some kind of magic power. "Hey! Look what I can do with just *these* ingredients!"

Honestly, that was a kind of magic. We felt cared for no matter what, and that was my mother's superpower. Without realizing it, we learned you *can* face anything.

When we got older, my parents started their own private investigation business. Mom had no secrets from Luke and me; we knew *exactly* what she and Dad did, but we didn't always know what was going to happen next. We took in women and children, often at pretty crazy hours, because my mom and dad wanted to keep them safe and make sure those people who were experiencing their worst hour knew someone genuinely cared what happened to them.

You never knew *who* or *how many* were going to be at the kitchen table in the morning, but at our house, you knew all were welcome. To see people coming from all sorts of chaos, violence, or other trouble and share a meal in peace is to understand how healing that can be.

There wasn't fancy food on our breakfast table. It might be eggs from our chickens or a breakfast casserole, maybe a bunch of toast and cereal. But seeing the way our guests would eat like it was the best meal they'd had in ages? That spoke to me.

My mom treated my brother and me like we were equal members of the household. We were part of the work she and my dad were doing to help others. And because there were always people in and out, there were no rules about our friends staying over. All were welcome.

Plus, if you haven't figured it out already, my family *loves* people, loves having friends around. That kind of energy attracts people who love people, and it just keeps feeding itself. For my mom, who loves to throw parties, *any* reason to have a get-together was good enough.

Mom and Dad always figured things out. We might not have had a lot of money, but my mom was determined we were going to be healthy. Maybe we couldn't load up at the grocery store, but they had a plan.

Dad decided we needed a garden. We were growing most of our vegetables in a 20-by-40-foot plot behind that ramshackle house. We had new potatoes, okra, squash, bell peppers, sugar snap peas, cauliflower, cabbage, beans, tomatoes, cucumbers, and onions. It was crazy! Those okra plants just gave and gave. There are so many things you can do with okra if you know what it is, and we do—gumbo, pickled, stewed, and fried, of course.

This was the beauty of how Mama raised me! However many of my friends might be there, or however many people were staying over seeking help, or however many friends had shown up to help us as we were trying to refurbish that little house, the best part of the day would be when Mom would say to all us kids, "Okay, go pick what you want for dinner."

We'd all go scrambling off the porch and into the garden knowing we were having the world's best stir-fry for dinner. We knew not to pick more than we'd eat, but we were all good eaters. And we knew it was going to taste so fresh.

Most kids don't want to eat their vegetables. Yuck!

Mama understood that too. Part of sending us down to the garden was to get us to simmer down and burn off some energy, but I promise: she knew what she was doing. Without ever saying a word, she was teaching us the value and goodness of the vegetables. We saw where they came from, watched—and, when we were old enough, helped—her clean them, chop them into pieces, and throw them all into a white-hot cast-iron skillet.

That sizzle! When the vegetables hit the pan? There'd be a cloud of steam, then this sound of the vegetables getting cooked against the iron. My dad is a cast-iron man, and even though this chapter's about my mom, that smile on his face, shaking whatever pan and tossing the vegetables as they cooked? Well, you know why she fell for him!

And then, voilà! The Magic Pick-Your-Stir-Fry Supper was done.

Whether we had any money or not, it didn't matter. Everyone got more than enough to eat. We also got so many vitamins, nutrients, and antioxidants—even though we didn't know what any of that was back then— without our parents ever having to beg, nag, or force us to eat our veggies.

TEACHING LESSONS WITHOUT MAKING THEM "LESSONS" WAS ANOTHER one of my mom's greatest talents. She knows things about people; most folks want to contribute and give back. And that principle greases my mom's entertaining wheels too.

She's always had a very simple rule: if you're eating, you're working! Even with those we were taking into our home, it was clear how grateful they were to be included in the process. It made them feel needed, not just like people in need. My mom would hand someone a knife or a bowl to shuck peas, or she'd ask them to set the table. She believes there's a job for everyone—and she knows how to match people with the right job, always. That way, everyone feels needed.

Today, when you go to her house for a party, especially when all the Ya-Yas are together, everyone's in the kitchen with a glass of whatever they're drinking—*and* a knife, or a spoon, or a spatula. It's all hands on deck to make the snacks happen.

Mom always says, "Nothing makes you part of the party quite like getting it started in the kitchen!"

It's true. Even now when my girlfriends or songwriter buddies come over, I may have the table set up so pretty, but don't think we're not chopping, or slicing, or mixing up a little something in the kitchen together first. This way, entertaining isn't an overwhelming production, it's just a bunch of friends being together and getting their hands a little busy. Making the decision to get together is never overwhelming when everyone pitches in.

Plus, when you've got something to do with your hands, you'd be surprised the things that come out of people's mouths. Confessions, secrets, news! Something you might not want to brag about, but we all want to hear. Something you're concerned about but are holding inside because you're afraid of bringing other people down. You get so focused on the task, what's in your heart just slips out.

Now that's the beauty of a pretty Bitchin' Kitchen. It's how I was raised—with my mom and her friends, and Nonny and her group too! Sometimes they'd even get everyone together just because they knew someone needed to talk, to make sure whoever needed to get it out there had somewhere to go and tell it all. Because the Bitchin' Kitchen takes all the pressure off and puts the focus on the heart and what you're cooking. It's the safest place you could ever hope to find.

Bev's
CHICKEN SALAD

SERVES 6 TO 8

2 cups shredded cooked rotisserie chicken, or any other leftover cooked chicken, cut into small chunks

1 cup finely chopped celery, tops included

1½ cups grated cheddar cheese

½ cup dried cranberries

¾ cup toasted, chopped pecans or sliced almonds

¾ cup mayonnaise, plus more as needed

Celery seed (optional)

IN a bowl, combine the chicken with the chopped celery, cheese, dried cranberries, and nuts. Stir in the mayonnaise until everything is coated, using more as necessary. Season with celery seed to taste, if you like, before serving.

Salsa = Love in a Jar

The other thing about growing your own vegetables: there's always a lot more than you can eat fresh or give away. Over the years, Mom would have every single counter and table covered with freshly sanitized crystal mason jars. Then we would turn the garden into all kinds of awesome! Even when the fall turned to winter, we'd have such abundance.

Some years, we'd put up quarts and quarts of spaghetti sauce. I close my eyes and can still see that bright fire-engine-red sauce on the shelf, flecked with green herbs, bits of onions, little pieces of garlic and carrots, and the tomatoes. It would smell so good, simmering all day. Months later, when Mom had a spaghetti dinner, the day we put up that sauce would all come back. She'd untwist the lid, and you'd hear that little "pop" and smile. You remembered sweat pouring down under your T-shirt and feeling all sticky and gross when you were in the thick of the work. But you also knew, anytime one of those jars opened in November or whenever, you were about to get a big ol' mouthful of slow-cooked tomatoes and summer sunshine. Twirl your fork and get the noodles covered in sauce. When you put that in your mouth, the taste would be better than anything you could get in any restaurant or in any jar from some fancy grocery store. Talk about magic.

Mom did that with *everything* in the garden. Literally, every color of the rainbow. Anything that was grown in our garden ended up on those shelves. Nothing was wasted ever. If you could put it in a jar, we did. Pickles, sauerkraut from the cabbage, beets, carrots, pickled okra. But maybe my favorite thing of all was her fresh-from-the-garden salsa!

When you grow up in Texas, salsa is the fifth condiment. Salt, pepper, ketchup, and mustard are what most people go to. But in Texas, we have an extra "something, something" that makes the difference. Salsa is what it's all about. On eggs in the morning and on anything else the rest of the day—except maybe dessert.

When the garden would be throwing off just too much abundance, you knew my mom would be out in the kitchen. She'd start chopping, brining, combining, and putting up salsa. Because she and Dad did all the gardening organically, that little patch of dirt would produce and produce and produce.

Let me tell you, there is nothing like the salsa that comes fresh out of the garden. Tomatoes, peppers, onions, jalapeños, a little salt, some cilantro, and lime. It was like the garden exploding in your mouth when you ate it. Nothing was fresher, brighter-tasting, or more delicious. Nothing said "party" to us like a bowl of Mama's fresh salsa on the table, and a bag of chips or a plate of vegetables. *That* was the signal. Get ready for fun, even if it was just the four of us cutting up and laughing.

Everyone in our family is also all about canning, so that made Mama's salsa a year-round proposition. We'd put up every last tomato from the vines, all the onions and the garlic. When winter came, it didn't matter if it was cold and gray outside—you'd open one of those mason jars and, suddenly, it was July all over again.

That was the beauty of how my parents and their friends raised us: we learned to waste nothing, enjoy every last bit, and appreciate the stuff that really matters. Guy Clark, the Texas songwriting legend, used to sing this song called "Homegrown Tomatoes." It was about all the ways you can enjoy them, but in the end it all came down to how in life the things that make you happy—like homegrown tomatoes or true love—you can't buy.

Kind of exactly like my mom's, my dad's, my nonny's, and my pop-pop's love. That's when you know you're doing it right—when a bowl of salsa you put up and a bag of chips turn your house into a party right there in the kitchen or on your back porch.

Bev's
GARDEN SALSA

MAKES 5 CUPS

1 bell pepper, coarsely chopped

1 large yellow onion, coarsely chopped

½ bunch cilantro, stems removed and leaves coarsely chopped

3 or 4 fresh tomatoes, coarsely chopped

1 (28-ounce) can crushed tomatoes

1 (10-ounce) can diced tomatoes with green chiles (I like Ro-Tel)

2 cloves garlic, minced

1 tablespoon fresh lime juice

2 large jalapeños, halved and seeded

1 tablespoon sugar

ADD the bell pepper, onion, a handful of cilantro, and the fresh tomatoes to a blender and blend until everything is finely chopped. Pour into a bowl and add the crushed tomatoes, diced tomatoes with chiles, garlic, and lime juice. Stir well.

PUT the jalapeños in the blender and blend until the desired texture. Start adding the chopped jalapeño, a little at a time, to your mix in the bowl until you get the heat you want. (The salsa will get a bit hotter as it sits.) When you get the heat right, stir in the sugar.

REFRIGERATE the salsa, covered, until ready to serve. It keeps for a *long* time!

4

PORCH PARTIES AND FAMILY FAVORITES FROM THE HOUSE THAT BUILT ME

▼▼▼▼▼▼▼▼▼▼▼▼▼▼▼▼▼▼▼▼▼▼▼▼

I grew up outside a pretty small town, Lindale, Texas. There were maybe 2,500 people when I was growing up and 212 churches in our county. People took high school football very seriously. Everybody pretty much knew everybody—and everybody's kids knew each other too.

Because we lived out in the country, when our friends came to visit they often stayed. It wasn't always by design, but we loved having our friends with us, and our house always sort of operated on the idea of "the more, the merrier." Mom never minded. She loved the energy of having people around, the laughter and the chatter. In some ways, all that friendship built the House That Built Me as much as the drywall and the cans of paint did. Those first few years we never knew who might drop by, but we were glad to see everyone who did.

It was during this time, when I was around six years old, that my mom started to develop her core group of friends. We'd moved to Lindale from Dallas after the oil crash; times were tight all over Texas, and my parents' private investigation business struggled. It was a time of rebuilding our lives and really leaning in to friends who would last a lifetime.

While we were living in a rental I barely remember, Mom would drive by a white farmhouse sitting off the road on her way home. It looked abandoned and needed some love, but Mom would ask God every day to

bring her this little house, so she could help heal it. One day an old farmer knocked on her door and asked if she was the lady who kept driving by his property. "Yes," she said, she was; she thought that house needed some love, and she wanted her family to provide it. And that's how the House That Built Me was leased to our family.

When we moved to the House That Built Me, which had been constructed on a sugarcane patch, sometimes my daddy would go sit out on this little hill just to take in the view. He'd sit there and stare at what God had created.

When you went up to that ramshackle house, with its one bathroom off the kitchen that didn't have a shower, only a claw-foot tub, you wouldn't notice any of that. All you'd see was this charming little jewel box of a home my mom created with a few sponges, a little bit of paint, and a headful of farmhouse-chic ideas.

You have to know this: the first time Nonny drove by and saw the place, she cried. It was all but condemned, but my mother had a vision. My mom with a vision is unstoppable. Room by room, she brought that dream of a sanctuary for her family to life. Even more than how it looked, she made those rooms a place where people would kick off their shoes, not because there was a fancy carpet, but because it felt so much like "home" in *every* sense of the word. People just wanted to stay awhile.

While we didn't have a lot of money, my parents always found a way to feed anyone who was around. Whether it was friends who'd come by with Sheetrock or tools my parents needed to work on the house, or people who *knew* my dad would take out a guitar and play a few classic country songs, or any number of families in trouble, there was always room at the table.

Mom had her ways, and so did her friends, who'd come by for the fun, to talk about their lives, or looking for advice. I can still see everyone out in the kitchen pulling a meal together and making sure we were all getting something to eat. The Magic Pick-Your-Stir-Fry Supper is part of that. When you've got a bunch of children—and grown-ups too—pulling dinner out of your garden is a pretty cost-efficient way to feed a crowd.

Everybody loved when my parents would fire up the grill and throw on some sausage, chicken, or whatever game my dad had gotten hunting and slather it with Paw Paw Sauce, something my mom's dad learned to make while serving in the National Guard. It's a little bit of everything, and that might be what makes it so good. Bell pepper, onion, brown sugar, ketchup, Worcestershire sauce, and mustard might sound like a strange combination, but put that mix on something and let it cook, and you're never going back. In a world of pouring barbecue sauce out of a bottle, this tastes like someone caring enough about you to mix up something special. No preservatives. No additives. No flavor enhancers. Just good ingredients that make anything they touch so much more than just a plain piece of meat or whatever kind of burger strikes your fancy.

We always have a batch of Paw Paw Sauce in a jar in my refrigerator because it's good, but also because it tastes like home. When I taste that sauce, it takes me back to that house every time. Beyond the friends and the food, there was the sound of my dad's guitar. When the day was done and we were all fed, people would stick around hoping he'd play. Sometimes other folks would pop in just for the chance to hear him. We could have thirty, forty people on the porch, in the yard, or in the house, visiting and enjoying the evening—and as time passed, other musicians joined in too.

I didn't quite know what it was about the music, but I was excited to hear it. It made me feel good, even the sad songs. When I was really little, I'd crawl into Dad's lap and just fall asleep, and he'd somehow go on playing. It was my baptism into music that I didn't even realize was happening. He just made everything sound so good, I wanted to be there.

At some point, he taught me to sing "Daddy's Hands" by Holly Dunn, and it became my "greatest hit." Three years in a row, third grade through fifth grade, he came to school and played guitar for me so I could sing in the talent show. But, to be honest, as much as I loved to sing, I would've almost rather listened back then.

Our house was the center of the universe for my mom and dad's friends and all their families. It was a place that folks gathered to do the important things of life: Be together. Share. Work together to get things done. Laugh. Cook. Teach their children the value of all those things. I can't count the number of times I watched my dad and his best friend, Rod, stand by the grill, flipping whatever they were making that night, joking, laughing, and just enjoying each other's company.

When Rod, Denise, and their kids spent the weekend at our place, we kids ran around like wild deer. That is the kind of joy and freedom that many kids don't get to have these days. And when it was time for dinner, we'd often gather in the House That Built Me for something simple, something that didn't take a lot of work and tasted better the longer it cooked.

Things take time. Cooking, fixing up old houses, and growing up—all things that happen in pieces. You never think about all the steps, because you're taking them. When a room would be done or a dish brought to the table, we loved whatever it was. The transformation wasn't what you thought about; you were struck by what you were about to taste or the new paint. More than patience, it's loving the process without even thinking about the process. Just keep doing the next thing, I've learned, because all those small things can add up to some pretty incredible things.

Paw Paw
SAUCE

MAKES 1 QUART

¼ cup vegetable oil

½ cup finely chopped green bell pepper

½ cup finely chopped yellow onion

2 cups ketchup

2 tablespoons mustard

2 tablespoons Worcestershire sauce

¼ cup light brown sugar

IN a skillet, heat the oil over medium high. Add the bell pepper and onion and sauté until tender and the onion is slightly translucent, about 5 minutes. Stir in the ketchup, mustard, Worcestershire, and brown sugar and bring to a boil. Reduce the heat to low and let simmer for 15 to 20 minutes, or longer if you'd like.

SERVE the sauce hot or cold. Leftovers can be stored in an airtight container in the refrigerator for up to a week.

Oven
BRISKET

SERVES 6 TO 8

Western-style barbecue seasoning or rub (I like Adkins)

1 whole USDA Choice or Prime beef brisket (10 to 12 pounds), untrimmed (using either Choice or Prime meat is very important for this recipe)

Kosher salt and freshly ground black pepper

1 large yellow onion, sliced

RUB the seasoning all over the brisket and lightly season with salt and pepper. Lay the brisket in a large foil pan, fat side up, and let sit at room temperature for 1 hour.

PREHEAT the oven to 300°F.

COVER the brisket with the onion, then add 1 cup water to the bottom of the pan. Cover tightly with foil and cook for 8 to 10 hours, until an instant-read thermometer inserted into the thickest part of the meat registers 200°F.

REMOVE the foil and let cool slightly in the pan. Transfer to a large cutting board. Using a sharp, serrated knife, cut the brisket in half and slice against the grain. Serve immediately, spooning juices over the slices.

Rick's
MAGIC BEANS

SERVES 6

6 slices of bacon, coarsely chopped

1 small yellow onion, chopped

1 (38-ounce) can Italian-style cut green beans, drained

1 tablespoon Worcestershire sauce

2 tablespoons maple syrup

Freshly ground black pepper

IN a skillet over medium heat, brown the chopped bacon and onion until very crispy, 5 to 7 minutes. Carefully pour off some of the bacon fat, but leave plenty to coat the skillet.

INCREASE the heat to medium-high and add the green beans, Worcestershire, and maple syrup to the skillet. Sauté for 2 to 4 minutes, stirring, then turn the heat down to a simmer. Let cook for 15 to 20 minutes more, 'til all the flavors blend together. Season with pepper before serving.

Daddy Lessons by Rick Lambert

SEASONING CAST IRON TO PERFECTION

My wife and daughter rescue dogs and cats. I rescue cast-iron pots, pans, and griddles. If I see a rusty old skillet or Dutch oven at a junk show or garage sale, it's like a sad-eyed puppy reaching out to me, saying, "Take me home." And without fail, I do!

Whether it's a "man thing," childhood memories of family meals, the pioneer spirit, or whatever, I love cast iron. Bev thinks I have an "unnatural attraction" to it. She's probably basing her opinion on the fact that she has, many times, walked into the kitchen to find me running my oil-covered hands over a newly seasoned pan while mumbling, in a doting and hushed tone, my admiration and love for the shiny black sheen that emanates from the surface.

Everyone who knows me can tell you about my cast-iron obsession. After all, I literally own hundreds of pounds of the stuff, including Dutch ovens, cornpone pans, oyster grillers, skillets, griddles of all sizes, and on and on and on.

Cast iron is all I ever use to cook. It makes me think of camping trips and deer-camp gatherings past and present. I am the cook at deer camp (on Miranda's Oklahoma farm), and the skillets that hang on the walls as beloved decorations have turned out many eggs, homemade biscuits, and the surprise cobblers I occasionally spring on my hunting-buddy family. Oh, and also the chicken-fried venison steaks that would never taste as good if they were not sizzled in my three-inch-deep "chicken fryer." They are served covered in gravy, which is made in the very same pan after the frying is done. The other hunters are all younger than I am, and, as their mentor, I have taught each one how to care for and nurture my beloved cast iron. Do they dare throw it into a sink of soapy water? NAY! What an abomination!

I'll proudly say that both of our children have adopted a reverence and love for the shiny kettles and skillets they grew up with. So that led to the following tutorial Miranda asked me to write, describing my tried-and-true method of seasoning cast iron. There are numerous ways to do this, but I think this one is the best—and so does my collection! You can now buy pre-seasoned cast iron, which comes "ready to cook," but only a pan that has fried eggs, potatoes, and bacon or cooked beans and cabbage will bring the true taste of your family heritage. That takes a while, but most good things usually do.

Let's start with one of those poor old rusty junk-store skillets looking for a good home. Some are only a little rusty, while some are so rusty that they have begun to "pit." Those unfortunates should be relegated to use for growing herbs on the back porch. Pitting prevents the pan from attaining sheen, slickness, and the nonstick surface you're looking for.

To start your journey to perfect cast iron, get a spray bottle filled with half white vinegar and half water. Shake it up and spray the entire pan: on the inside, the outside, and all over the handle. Set the pan on a towel for fifteen minutes, then rinse it with cold water. A good bit of rust will come off. I repeat this process three times, and each time more rust disappears. Next, dry the pan and use a soapy steel

wool pad to scrub off any remaining stubborn rust. This is the one and *only* time you will use soap on your cast iron. Some folks might argue that last point, but this is my method (and my tutorial), and I believe in it. Rinse the pan with hot water and wipe dry.

Preheat your oven to 350°F. This is where the love begins, kind of like the lotion part of a massage. Choose any oil that you prefer: canola, vegetable, grapeseed, etc. My personal preference is Crisco shortening or bacon grease (which I keep in a small pot on top of the stove). Hand-rub a thin layer of oil all over the entire surface of the pan: top, bottom, handle, and rim. You can always use a folded-up paper towel or brush it on, but I find that using my hands works best, and it also starts the "bonding" with my new friend. And I believe my new friend remembers when called to duty on a hot burner!

After applying the oil, put your buddy upside down on the middle rack of your oven. Place a flat cookie sheet or baking pan underneath to catch any drippings. Bake it for one

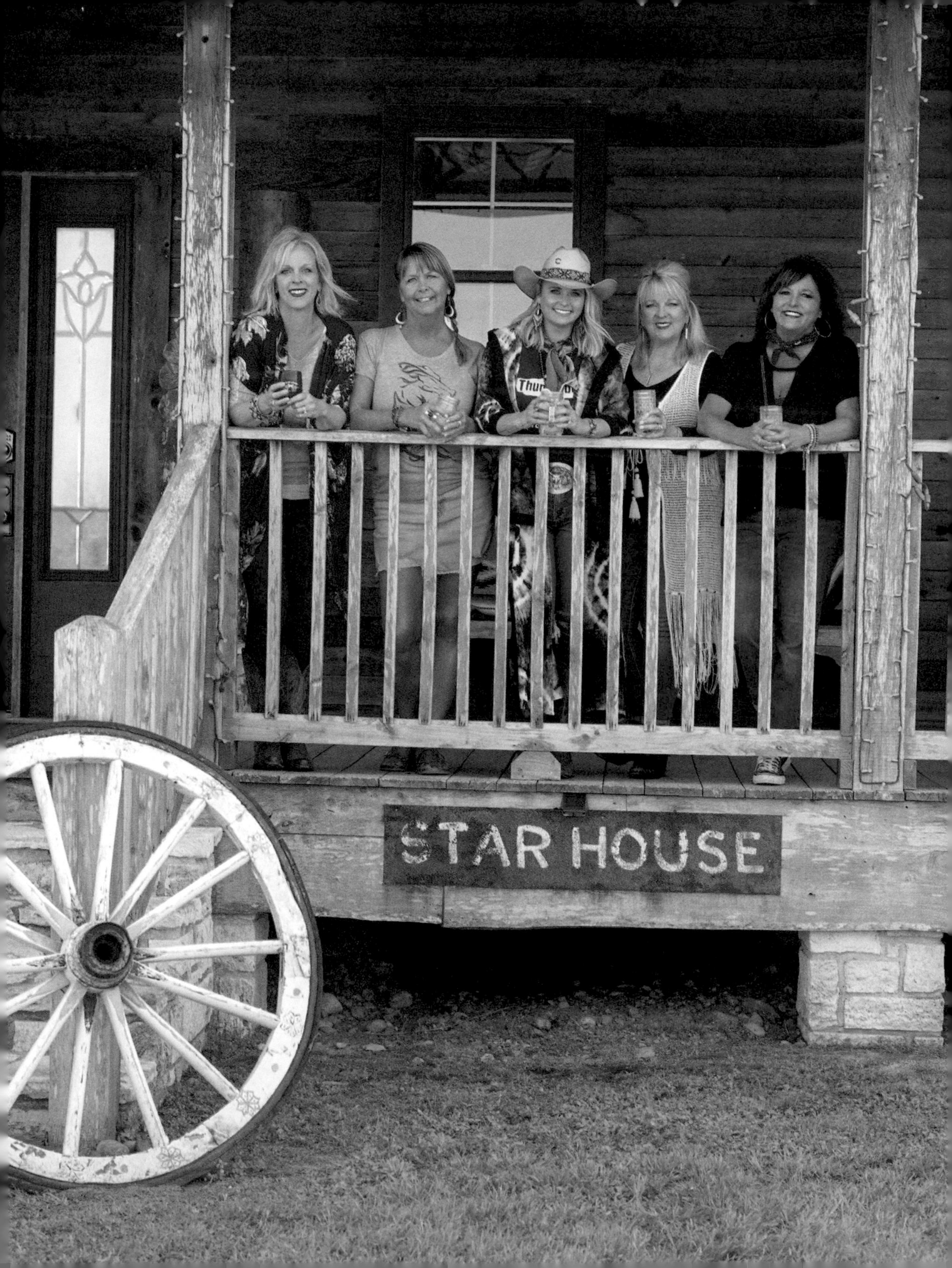
STAR HOUSE

hour, then take it out and let it cool. I usually do this three times before the sheen starts to come through. At the end of the baking, put another very small amount of oil in the pan before storing it away. (I proudly hang mine on an overhead pot rack for all to see.)

Now it's ready to start cooking!

Sometimes after cooking in cast iron, you can just wipe it out really well with a paper towel, rub a thin layer of oil on it, and heat it up on a burner or in the oven to get it clean. For stubborn food pieces that stick, you can simply boil a little water in the pan to loosen them up, then scrape off the food pieces. Then dry and season your pan once again.

Never put cast iron away wet or damp. Always remember that oil is your friend and ally! Tomato-based recipes sometimes burn the pans due to the acidity, so just give them some special oily attention after cooking things like marinara sauce.

Here's my last tip, and it's a big one! Every so often, cut up some raw potatoes and fry a batch in your cast-iron skillet, pot, or Dutch oven. Something about the starch in the potatoes helps seal the pores in the metal and will make your trusted (not rusted) friend really shine. Then you can simply wipe it out, tell it that you sincerely love it, and put it away! Plus, you get to enjoy some fried potatoes too.

5

MINE'S PRETTIER

▼▼▼▼▼▼▼▼▼▼▼▼▼▼▼▼▼▼▼▼▼▼▼▼▼

The Sisterhood of the Traveling Casserole Dish

My mother's friends always arrived with slow cookers, pans, Tupperware containers, and Ziploc bags full of goodness that all just jumbled together. Nobody really planned or noticed it, but Mom, Neicy, Vicki, and Heidi fell into this rhythm of friendship that in a lot of ways has become the World Series of dips, comfort food, and showing up for each other for just about everything.

It started in our house, but at this point, anywhere those four go, trouble, high spirits, and an electric skillet follow. They've got rocking-the-kitchen down to a science. And if they're eating—or drinking—and you want to get in on it, they'll look around, see what needs chopping, and put a knife in your hand. No one is ever left out if they want in, which is one of the coolest things about these women. You'll hear my mom joke, "We've got forty, fifty fingers? We can do this!"

It's hilarious watching them. Even though every single one of them is a really good cook, each has their individual strengths. If it's cookies, that's Vicki's department. If it's Cajun, that's for Neicy to handle. Heidi is all about those hot crackers and her pimento cheese. My mom is the Queen of Chicken Salad. And they all know their way around a tray of deviled eggs. So if you're coming around, it's best to come hungry.

When I think about kitchen stuff, I always think about my mom's white casserole dish with flowers that were the prettiest shade of blue—not just flowers, but cornflowers. She and my dad received it as a wedding present. Innovative at the time, a Corelle casserole could go from refrigerator to oven to table. It looked pretty enough to serve in, and that was important to my mom.

To us, though, it was a big deal because chicken spaghetti might be coming out of it. Chicken spaghetti! Let's talk about the creamy goodness: cream of mushroom soup, cream of chicken soup, a can of Ro-Tel tomatoes, noodles, sour cream, and cheese, all blended together with pieces of chicken. It's so easy, especially in these times of rotisserie chicken. Think of it as an instant hot meal or total comfort food. Same thing with lasagna, layered enchiladas, King Ranch chicken, or baked beans with bacon over the top. That little casserole held so many of our favorite things, but even more, it's Mom to me. It's also now the place that cooked dips are made in, because it can go to the table and keep it warm, waiting for our chips.

Rarely was a casserole used to feed just four people. These women were experts at feeding big groups of hungry people. It's a little bit crazy when they get into casserole mode: chicken and dumplings for a crowd; lasagna in massive amounts.

And it's not just dinner casseroles or dips either.

Squash casseroles. Sweet potato casseroles. Green bean casseroles. A potato salad, too, especially a German potato salad that some people heat up. Scalloped potatoes. Hash brown casseroles are a new entry, but, man, they are gone first anytime they're served.

There's also this pride in the actual dishes we use. Nonny got to where she'd make her casseroles in those giant, heavy tin disposable pans. She'd say, "Well, I made one for you to take home" or "It freezes beautifully." Nonny was all about the leftovers and the fact that these things are usually better the next day.

Mom would rather die than use a big tin pan. I've seen her go to Walmart and buy an inexpensive casserole dish if she's taking something to someone's house who she doesn't know very well. She wants to present properly. All the Ya-Yas do.

When the casserole dishes start stacking up, you don't have to panic. These ladies tag their dishes like animals in the wild kingdom. You will find one of those return address stickers you get in the mail taped to the bottom of the dishes, or a piece of masking tape will be on the lid with someone's name written in Sharpie marker. That's how serious our people take the food they bring, and what they bring it in.

Plus, there are rules that are attached to what goes in a casserole. My mom says, "You can't travel with a juicy bean." And it's a fact. You can't. You have to know this, or you will have a mess in your back seat or someone's lap. Pinto beans with a lot of juice won't work; black-eyed peas are the same way. There's a line. *Don't* cross it.

Calico beans? Now that's something that travels! You take four kinds of beans—butter beans, navy beans, a couple others fry up some bacon with a little onion, and then cook up some ground meat. Let that simmer before putting it in your casserole dish to finish cooking or travel. All the colors make it look like calico fabric, but don't let the name fool you. It's a real stick-to-your-ribs, cowboy kind of meal. My mom just loves making it; she says it's a real chuckwagon dinner that'll keep you full until morning.

Another truth: there is no casserole as delicious as the breakfast casserole. If you're lucky, you'll have a friend like Neicy. She brings her French toast casserole when she visits, and it's the greatest morning-after *ever*. That is having a bite of New Orleans first thing in the morning, and it lifts your spirits. Literally, as you pull that out of the refrigerator and pop it in your oven, the power of the casserole is never more obvious.

The Sisters of the Traveling Casserole Dish are obviously my mom and her friends, but it's also a state of mind. You might well be part of our tribe too. It's how you come together, make friends, figure out how to take care of other people by feeding their bodies and their souls. And it's the spirit in your heart. You don't even need to speak English to be "filled with the spirit," because it travels beyond our houses, Airstreams, and the places we ramble. Obviously, the Ya-Yas come out on the road with us, come to the big events, but traveling around the world has shown each of us this: everyone who cooks cooks from their heart.

In 2010 we did a girls' trip to Italy to see the wine country and all that beautiful land. Every one of us was struck by the way people a world away love so many of the same things we do. The Italian people are as proud of their countryside as Texans are of the horizon line and the Guadalupe River.

While we were there we wanted to take a cooking class. What could be more us? We were in Chianti, and the kitchen was on top of this mountain. You should've seen all these Texas women "ascending the mountain," all in the name of pasta and red sauce! When we got there, all these Italian mee-maws, really darling little old ladies, were going to teach us how to make *their* version of soul food. Though we barely spoke each other's language, we completely understood what those women were telling us.

To see them working the same way we did also showed us how universal cooking together and feeding people is. They had what they did down to a science, just like the Ya-Yas do with their stuff. They were mixing the flour, water, and eggs, then kneading it just right; showing us the proper consistency of the dough, so we'd know when we got home. Then they were putting it into the machine, and they pulled us in just like Mom does with people in her kitchen. They had us help cut the pasta. We were catching it as it came off the line, cutting it up and having a ball.

Then we were making red sauce, slow-cooking to let the flavors settle. For all the sauce we made at our house growing up, this was a whole other way. But like at our house, it was also the simplest stuff.

We drank lots and lots of wine too! We were in Chianti, after all. When we were done, we ate everything we'd made that day for dinner. Let me tell you, the difference between fresh, homemade pasta and anything else is massive. The flavor and the texture are so full. For a kid raised on noodle casseroles, homemade pasta is like seeing the pyramids of lusciousness.

Brendan, my husband, was raised around Italians (he's actually Dominican and Irish). Being a full-on kitchen daredevil, he has made fresh pasta a few times. That daredevil's in his blood. But when you try it on your own, be prepared for the stumble. For us, the first time we made it, we realized too late we didn't have a drying rack. Wet fresh pasta was everywhere, so in the true Ya-Ya spirit, I put some plastic wrap over a few hangers and just hung that up to dry. Again, just because it's not what the cookbook says doesn't mean you can't make it work. Think about what you need to have happen—get the pasta hung up to dry—and you'll be surprised what idea pops in your head.

Sisters are everywhere! Sometimes when you find one, it'll make you just stop in your tracks. One of the most thrilling sisters I've ever encountered was the late, great Loretta Lynn! Miss Loretta was a true pioneer woman, not just as a songwriter and a legend but also as a make-it-happen superstar who also knew how to fry a chicken and make a piecrust from scratch. Remember those Crisco commercials? *Come on!*

In 2010 I recorded "Coal Miner's Daughter" with Loretta and Sheryl Crow, another hero of mine. Both of those women cut paths that were unthinkable, had success on their terms, and managed never to lose a speck of their womanliness.

Going down to Hurricane Mills, Tennessee, to shoot the video at Loretta's ranch was one of the most important days of my life. To be in her world making music is the stuff you don't dare dream about. I was overwhelmed with emotion the entire day, and I still well up a bit thinking about it. I actually got to sit in Loretta Lynn's kitchen, listening to her tell stories about her husband and kids. She was incredibly funny and so true and honest that it's almost hard to absorb. And this is why she was absolutely part of the sisterhood!

That day, she told me the most hilarious story about her husband, Doo, coming home and smelling of liquor. He sat himself down at the table and said, "Where's dinner?" In true Loretta style, she said, "Here it is . . ." and threw the whole skillet at him! She didn't say whether she hit him or not, but if I had to guess, I'd say she barely missed. Now, if that's not a real country song, I don't know what is. But that's why we loved her so much. Loretta Lynn lived her songs. She was as authentic as could be, just like the country music I was raised on.

Between takes she showed Sheryl and me around her house, which was everything you'd hope it would be. Even more exciting, she had a collection of salt and pepper shakers just like mine. If those were cool enough for Loretta Lynn, you know you're on to something pretty cool.

That's the thing about this sorority. We don't get caught up in the big stuff. The rules are basic: the simpler, the better, and the more, the merrier. What can you create where you are, without making too much of a fuss or missing all the fun?

Recently, Brendan and I were going over to our friend's house for dinner. There were a bunch of us getting together, and some of us have kids. Beyond never wanting to come empty-handed, I figured, "What would those kids like to eat?" In our house, you never asked what was for supper, because whatever it was, you were gonna eat it (or not). But I'm still a big Velveeta-and-shells kind of girl, which means I get how kids have certain things they just love.

We were out at our farm, so I couldn't really run over to the store. Looking in the refrigerator to see what we had, I got cooking! With a page from the kitchen-sink playbook, I browned up some ground meat, poured in some tomatoes, grabbed a can of mixed vegetables and a can of corn. I added some cheese, mixed it up, and let it settle for a few minutes on low. I scooped it all into a casserole, crunched up some potato chips to use for a crispy topping—and we were ready to go!

Those kids loved it! The grown-ups did too. All we had left was an empty dish. Sisters of the Traveling Casserole Dish did it again!

Potato SALAD

1¼ pounds new potatoes, cut into 1-inch cubes

½ teaspoon kosher salt, plus more for boiling

½ cup finely chopped green onions

½ cup grated cheddar or American cheese

2 hard-boiled large eggs, chopped

¼ cup sweet pickle relish

½ cup mayonnaise

1 tablespoon mustard

½ teaspoon freshly ground black pepper

½ teaspoon paprika

PLACE the potatoes in a pot of cold salted water. Bring to a boil over high heat, then reduce the heat to medium, and cook until the potatoes are tender, 10 to 15 minutes.

DRAIN the potatoes and let cool completely, then transfer to a bowl. Add the green onions, cheese, eggs, and relish. Gently stir in the mayonnaise and mustard to combine. Season with the salt and pepper. Chill in the fridge until cold, about 2 hours. Sprinkle with the paprika before serving.

Old Timer's
GREEN BEAN CASSEROLE

SERVES 6

Cooking spray

4 tablespoons (½ stick) unsalted butter

2 cups cornflakes

¼ cup all-purpose flour

¼ teaspoon kosher salt

¼ teaspoon freshly ground black pepper

2 (14.5-ounce) cans cut green beans, drained

1 cup sour cream

2 cups grated Longhorn-style block cheese

PREHEAT the oven to 400°F. Grease a 10 x 6-inch casserole dish with cooking spray.

IN a skillet, melt 2 tablespoons of the butter. Pour the melted butter in a bowl and toss with the cornflakes to coat. Set aside.

MELT the remaining 2 tablespoons butter in the skillet. Add the flour and cook, stirring constantly, until browned. Season with salt and pepper. Remove from the heat and add the green beans, stirring to coat. Stir in the sour cream until well combined.

POUR the green bean mixture into the prepared casserole dish. Top evenly with grated cheese and buttered cornflakes. Bake for 30 minutes, until browned and bubbly.

Slow Cooker BREAD PUDDING

SERVES 8 TO 10

3 large eggs

⅔ cup packed light brown sugar

2 teaspoons ground nutmeg

2 tablespoons ground cinnamon

1 cup heavy cream

1 cup whole milk

2 teaspoons vanilla extract

GLAZE

½ cup heavy cream

1 cup granulated sugar

½ cup (1 stick) unsalted butter, melted

8 cups cubed French bread

½ cup butterscotch baking chips

2 cups pecans, chopped

Cooking spray

Whipped cream (page 207), for serving (optional)

½ cup (1 stick) unsalted butter, melted

½ cup whiskey or dark rum

IN a large bowl, whisk together the eggs, brown sugar, nutmeg, and cinnamon. Add the heavy cream, milk, vanilla, and melted butter. Add the bread cubes and toss until completely coated. Stir in the butterscotch chips and pecans.

COAT a large slow cooker with cooking spray, then pour in the bread mixture. Cover and cook on low for 2 hours, until the center is firm and a knife inserted in the center comes out clean.

MEANWHILE, make the glaze: In a small pot, combine the cream, granulated sugar, and melted butter. Cook over medium-low heat until the sugar is dissolved. Do not let boil. Remove from the heat and stir in the whiskey or dark rum.

POUR half the glaze over the bread pudding and reserve the other half for serving. Top with whipped cream, if desired, to serve.

Deviled Eggs

THE ONE THING EVERYONE AGREES ON!

No matter what we're doing, the time of day, the place, or the reason for getting together, when we have people over or do anything, deviled eggs are a part of it. I'm not sure why exactly, beyond that they're so delicious, but it's *never* a party—or anything else—without them.

Mom, Heidi, Neicy, Vicki: every single one has tricks that make their deviled eggs special. None of them will tell you what it is. After a while, you just accept it. Accept it and enjoy it.

It's the simplest thing. Hard-boiled eggs, split 'em in two, scoop out the yolks, and go to town. The basics are basic: a little mayo, a little vinegar, maybe some mustard, a little bit of red pepper. Whip it up with a fork until it's fluffy and light. Then gently scoop the mixture back into the yolk hole and dust it with a little paprika.

Some fancy people use a pastry bag and "pipe" the filling into the depression in each egg half. Or you can use a decent-weight plastic bag with a corner cut off. But any small spoon or spatula will get it done. Figure out how much filling you have, then portion out accordingly.

Few things look as "Let's go on a picnic" or "Here's to a new day" as deviled eggs. Two mouthfuls if you're hungry, three or four bites if you're being polite.

Deviled eggs are a big deal, and people from the South understand. You meet people from other parts of the country, they don't get what the fuss is all about. Why would anyone need to have special plates to put your eggs on? For my mom and her crew, though, not only do they all have special deviled egg plates, but Heidi and Vicki also have both regular ceramic plates *and* melamine plates for when we go glamping. Even more awesome—or crazy, depending on how you see it—the Fischer sisters have special carrying cases to pack up their eggs and go visiting, because when you take your deviled eggs properly serious, that's just part of it.

It's amazing how filling they can be without ruining your appetite.

If you're killing time while you're making dinner, they're fantastic. Or if everyone's listening to music and catching up with the hometown gossip, they'll tide you over and keep you sober until it's time for the actual meal.

They're a staple of church potlucks and picnics, though some places call 'em dressed eggs or salad eggs because they don't want the devil anywhere around. Ironically, the term, which goes back more than a hundred years, was coined to denote food that is very spicy, often because of the vinegar and cayenne in most deviled egg recipes.

SHHHH! Here's a little secret: as delicious as every one of the Ya-Yas' eggs are, Vicki is the undisputed queen of the deviled egg. Between the seasonings and the way she whips her yolks, there's this indescribable thing that hooks you. But don't believe me. Here's the recipe. Find out for yourself. Warning: be sure you make the whole dozen eggs. They'll be gone quicker than you'd ever imagine.

Vicki's DEVILED EGGS

MAKES 24 HALVES

1 dozen large eggs

1 teaspoon baking soda

½ cup chopped green olives

½ cup mayonnaise

1 teaspoon mustard

1 teaspoon freshly ground black pepper

Paprika

PLACE the eggs in a pot and cover with cold water. Add the baking soda. Bring to a boil and set a timer for 10 minutes. When the timer goes off, immediately take the pot off the heat. Drain and rinse the eggs under cold water, then peel.

SLICE the eggs in half lengthwise and carefully scoop out the yolks into a bowl. Mash the yolks with a fork, then add the olives, mayonnaise, mustard, and pepper. Stir to combine. Transfer the yolk mixture to a pastry bag with a large tip and squeeze some yolk mixture into each egg white half. (If you don't have a pastry bag, scoop the mixture into a gallon-size zip-top bag, snip the corner off, and *voilà*! Ya-Ya magic!) Sprinkle with paprika. Let the deviled eggs chill in the fridge for at least 4 hours or overnight for best results.

6

ROAD TRIPPIN',
BOOBS, AND TUBES

▼▼▼▼▼▼▼▼▼▼▼▼▼▼▼▼▼▼▼▼▼▼▼▼▼▼▼▼▼▼

Trips, Chips, and Good Times

When I was growing up, we had all kinds of fun. We'd go camping old-school–style. This was long before there was glamping. We'd take little road trips, sometimes to visit friends around the state or go see music. But the biggest, best trip of all was when we'd go tubing down the river. We used to call it "boobs and tubes." We still do, actually. It's one of those fun things to do when it doesn't matter who you are, how old you are, or where you came from. Once you're in the tube, everyone's the same. It's all systems go for the best day!

Here's the basic recipe for a good time, or at least a good time on the Guadalupe. And let me show you the proper way to drop its name: Gwah-DAH-loop . . . When you say it like that, you sound like you're from 'round here.

Guadalupe Good-Time Recipe

1. Tube *all* day.
2. Drink.
3. Take a nap.
4. Gather chairs around the lawn, camper, firepit, or wherever you may be.
5. Break out the snacks, the cold drinks, and your appetite.
6. Let my dad—or someone you know—start picking.
7. Join in!

Now *that's* a recipe for some *real* country fun! You float like Alan Jackson on the "Chattahoochee," splashing and laughing, then you come on in, dry off, rest up, and do it all over again. We were spoiled 'cause we had my daddy to provide the soundtrack. But even recorded music will do—play Death-by-iPod, or now I guess Death-by-iPhone. It's a great game where you try to keep topping each other's choice for saddest song, best drinking tune, greatest kiss-off, or whatever you're feeling.

Floating the Guadalupe is what all today's country guys are singing about. Only *we* do it. We've done it my whole life. My mom even floated the river when she was six and a half months pregnant with me, so you could say I was tubing even before I was born. There's nothing like good ol' boys, rednecks, and other sundry Texans in white water. We just love it that much. I remember being six years old, riding in a tube with my brother. He was just a baby, and it was just the two of us in our own tube. Talk about feeling like a grown-up.

For us, this is a family tradition that's been going on forever. And it's a trip to bring along the family you choose, like Denise and her kids and anyone else we drag with us. We're still doing it; at one point, it grew to be 112 people. Vicki, Denise, and I finally had to cut the numbers down, unbeknownst to my mom. But nothing will stop us: we're still floating . . .

And we were big campers too. Everything to us was an adventure, so river trips were *two* adventures in one. Cooking out for breakfast was one more fun thing we didn't do at home. When we were little, Neicy taught us to make shake-'em-up omelets: you cracked your eggs into a zip-top bag, added whatever filling—peppers, cheese, mushrooms, bacon, sausage, etc.—and shook it up, then rolled the bag to squeeze out most of the air and sealed it up. You wrote your name on it and dropped it into a pot of boiling water that was sitting in the campfire. Before too long, it was cooked! Open that bag: you had an omelet.

We lived forty-five minutes from *any* water, so going to the river was a big deal. I remember asking my dad on one of our trips, when we'd gotten pretty dirty, "Where do we take our shower?"

He laughed, handed us each a bar of Irish Spring, and pointed to the water. What could be more "wilderness adventure" than running down to the water with that green-and-white soap in our hands, jumping up and down, splashing each other, and lathering up? Looking back, I laugh about how basic some of this stuff was, but it felt so exotic then.

We didn't have the money. Disney? That was waaaaaaaay too expensive for us. Six Flags in Dallas? We went occasionally, but, honestly, we probably would've rather been out on the river with the grown-ups, whooping it up and having a big time. When you've got two kids and a blue-collar salary, there isn't always a lot of money for "extras." Looking back, I don't believe a theme park would've been as much fun. I didn't know the history of where we were or what the river meant; I only knew how much fun we were having. We didn't need the theme park or the roller coasters—we were having too big a time right where we were.

The first thing you have to know about the Guadalupe is that the water moves very fast, so it is very clean. The speed keeps it clear and pretty. The second thing you have to know is that it is ice cold *all* the time. Literally, it feels like ice water. Your initial launch into the water is a good little shocker!

You need to be ready, or it'll knock the breath out of you. Sometimes—if you want to be tricky—you don't tell a first-timer about this, and they yelp. But on a hot day in Texas, that cool water feels so good.

It's always different, every time you float it. When the water's high, it'll take you about three hours to float it—and the world just passes you by. If the water's low, which is more likely, it can take as long as eight hours, Depending on where and how low the water is, in some parts you may actually have to get out of your tube and walk. The river is different from year to year. Over time, it has evolved. John Prine observed how old rivers and trees grow wilder—and he's right. But some things about this river, they're always the same.

When we were little, our parents let us have room just to be. My mom would tell us, "If you get too far out in front, grab hold of a tree branch and wait 'til I can see you."

We didn't weigh very much, and she knew that could happen. But the trees—these amazing bald cypresses and willows—line the banks of the Guadalupe; they hang so weightlessly over the water, so it was nothing to just reach up, grab a handful of vines, and wait for everyone else to catch up.

Word of caution: it gets a little snaky near the edge! When I was seventeen—in my Walmart two-piece string bikini that I had *no* business wearing—a snake fell out of a tree onto my tube. I swear to you, I walked on the water like Jesus, I was so scared. I screamed so loud I probably scared the snake to death. I bolted straight up out of the water and started walking. I laugh now, but it was terrifying. That's the thing about these trips: stuff happens. It makes for a great story, but I'll also never forget that surge of adrenaline.

There are a few other things you *need* to know. You need to wear river shoes, or just basic dollar store sneakers you can leave behind. The river is muddy and slimy on the bottom, plus there are rocks, and you never know what someone may've thrown in the water.

We always did a dollar store run before we got there. You need aloe vera, too, because you're gonna get tube rash! Aloe gel is the one thing that makes it feel better. We're talking raw black rubber in the Texas heat, because most of us get our tire tubes from the tire shop. Now there's a company called Texas Tubes, where you get picked up in an old-school bus that's all painted up. We've been doing this long enough, we're old school. You just need to know that sometimes there are plastic pieces that can pinch the hell out of you, so get that aloe vera.

You're going to want a second tube for your cooler. You take a bunch of twine, make a few loops across the bottom part of the opening, and set your cooler in there. You ice it down, drop in your beer (or Capri Suns for the kids), then set it off the edge to get it floating. You have to run and jump into your own tube before the cooler takes off with your drinks. You were gonna do that anyway, but once that cooler tube starts moving, there can be *no* second thoughts. Talk about luxury, though, just floating down the river with your cooler in a tube next to you, the sun and trees overhead, *and* all your friends with you.

With time, we got smarter too. My mom went and bought one of those three-gallon plastic jugs with a spout. She loaded it up with muddled fruit and wine and just tossed it in the tube, pulling it along with us. She had a sangria tube. It was fantastic!

When I was eighteen, I remember putting a few Zimas in my cooler, then dropping some Jolly Ranchers in them. I thought I was just living the life! And you know, I was.

I also have a vision of Denise from that trip. Man, was she something else in her gold string bikini. I can see her holding her tube, pulling it over the rocks like some kind of queen!

There's one last thing about floating that you should know: you're gonna see some parts. Whether it's shorts slipping off from the water weighing 'em down or a bikini top wiggling where it shouldn't, you're gonna see a little more of your friends than you ever expected. That's just how it is goes.

up, it's *on*! All the dips, the snacks, the deviled eggs, and whatever else comes out of those coolers. Grab a bag of chips, or veggies if you're trying to be healthy, and have at it.

There's also some incredible cooking going on, a few of our particular kind of delicacies that taste even better in the "wild." My dad, who is the King of Cast Iron, has all these tricks that make camping-out food even better. We knew when we hit the river or a campground, there would be plates full of Campfire Casserole and Coffee Can Cobbler.

For Campfire Casserole, tear several pieces of heavy-duty foil into about 12 x 12-inch squares. You will need two pieces per person. In the middle of one piece, add raw hamburger meat, diced potatoes (any kind), sliced onions, sliced carrots, or small corn on the cob if you like. Season the mixture with salt and pepper. Fold and roll the foil around the food to form a tight packet. Put the packet seam side down on the second piece of foil and wrap and roll it again. Throw all the packets onto a hot fire and let cook for 45 minutes. Remove, unfold, and eat right out of the foil! We served it with ketchup or Paw Paw Sauce. Slow-cooked, with all the flavors melting into each other, it's almost a self-realizing dish. When you take a forkful of that, you can't help but feel all warm inside.

Coffee Can Cobbler works off the same kind of use-what-you-got engineering. When we first started camping, we literally made it in a metal

coffee can! But for more conventional situations, it cooks in a cast-iron Dutch oven. You can find the recipe on page 97.

THE THINGS YOU CAN DO WITH JUST A LITTLE, WITH STUFF THAT'S SO everyday you don't ever think about what kind of magic you might make with it? It's amazing. It's delicious. It's perfect.

Going on the river, we'd usually end up close to Gruene Hall, which in Texas music is one of the holiest places of them all. Built in 1878, it's a plain white wood-slat building, but it's six thousand square feet of the oldest continually running dance hall in Texas. It's been in movies, hosted ZZ Top's documentary, been listed on the National Registry of Historic Places. It's also where many young artists got started. We knew that. Everyone in Texas, really, knows that.

When I was thirteen, my mother and I went inside one afternoon. There was a guy playing a guitar in the corner, a couple people having a beer at the bar, but it was basically empty. That time of day, people are out on the water or resting up for later that night. My mom, who's as big a dreamer as I am, was with me as we walked up in front of that stage. All of a sudden, she turned and looked me right in the eye. She said, "You get up on that stage, and you claim it in the name of Jesus!" She was *not* fooling, because my mother takes her faith very seriously—and she knew what this place meant to me as a girl who loved music and as a songwriter who wanted to make her mark. We didn't really, truly understand what it was going to take to make it, but we knew exactly what this place and that stage meant to so many artists we loved.

I'll never forget that moment. Mom put her hands right on my boots and said, "Lord Jesus, we claim this stage in Your name, in Your glory, through Miranda's voice. Amen."

When you walk out into a space like that, with that kind of a blessing, you feel it. You know something's upon you. I could almost feel all the people who'd been there before me: Willie Nelson, Merle Haggard, George

Strait, Jerry Jeff Walker; the booker for the room, Tracie Ferguson, wanted to do original music, and really important Texas writer/artists Townes Van Zandt, Robert Earl Keen, Nanci Griffith, Jimmie Dale Gilmore, Bruce Robison, and Lyle Lovett were all part of what sets Gruene Hall in history. That was a lot of power to draw on.

Even when I was thirteen, I went up there not to be a cute kid with a dream, but to be a young woman who fully intended to one day take that stage for my own. My mom knew it when she sent me up to stand onstage. It was three o'clock in the afternoon. I'm not sure anybody even saw us doing it. But this wasn't for anybody other than us. I knew I wasn't ready yet, but it lit a real fire in me. In that moment, standing there, I knew *this* was my future—absolutely and always, whatever it took.

When I think about headlining Gruene Hall six years later, it makes me shake my head and smile. Everywhere I go in Texas, I have these memories.

It's so much a part of who I am, where I've been. I take it with me. Even today, when we headline the Whitewater Amphitheater, which we've done for the last several years, I smile. Yes, we're up there rocking out, playing these songs, and bringing that kick-ass attitude to New Braunfels, but I'm also on that stage with my back to the Guadalupe River flowing by.

Those river floats cemented a lot of extended family. But they're also *a lot*—a lot of people, noise, and planning. They inspired our core group to break out and do something on our own. We thought, with our Airstream convoy and get-it-done attitude, why couldn't the girls take it on the road? (Trick question: we knew we could.)

And so the glamps began. These are totally footloose trips where we hitch our Airstreams and hit the road. Sometimes it's not even about where we're going but about being together and away from it all. No makeup, no worrying about how you look—though, with this crew, you can count on everyone looking like we were meant to be here.

To give you a clue how serious we are about these glamping trips: once, when it had been too long since we had a road trip and I couldn't get away because of work, the Ya-Yas decided to bring the glamp to me! Mom and her friends literally loaded up their Airstreams and drove straight to Nashville. They couldn't stand to see me missing something we all loved so much. They arrived, and we set up in my front yard out at the farm.

Whatever or however you need to get away with your people, never make it so hard that you can't make it happen. That's another bit of my mama's wisdom I'd like to make sure you make your own.

With that out of the way, let's talk about glamping. The basics: It's about being together. Food, while not the focus, is essential. We can all build a fire, but these ladies don't go anywhere without their electric skillets or their slow cookers. You'd be amazed at what they can do with a few basic household appliances.

Mom and Heidi especially, but all of them really, bring whatever they think they might need. When they come to shows and tailgate, their cars are loaded. I joke, "How long are you staying?" because they're so packed. Mom jokes, "Just bringing the pantry—and the party—with me." Plus, it's easier if you have what you need. She bought something she found on TV that boils water in a minute! Talk about a good thing to have. I get annoyed with all the gadgets, but I get it. The cooking is a lot easier with the gear these women bring with them—which means more time for eating and fun!

We all pack our coolers and refrigerators for three, four, five days and don't look back. We *know* what we're doing, how to delegate who's bringing what for maximum yumminess. When there's a glamp coming up, the text chains among the crew are pretty hilarious. My mom has a championship deviled egg carrier that holds twenty-four eggs. Princess V has melamine cupcake towers specifically for traveling. Oh, and we have a road case that turns into an actual bar. We set it up so we can have proper cocktails wherever we go.

We bring all the favorites: Mom's chicken salad, Heidi's hot crackers and pimento cheese, dips and dips and more dips. We love the trucker snacks: sausage balls, jerky. All stuff you can make ahead. Mom'll bring coleslaw, Vicki'll bring her potato salad and chili, April brings sausage-and-cheese dip, Neicy brings her corn dip and some of those Mexican sausage corn muffins, plus something Cajun. I bring the charcuterie and trucker snacks.

We don't do big meals; they take up too much time. Who wants to be that kind of full? We like light bites, things that are easy when it's just us girls. You'd be amazed at how far a charcuterie board, or even a bunch of celery and carrot sticks, maybe some slices of cucumbers and green, red, or yellow peppers, can go with some dip.

For us, "easy" is a good word. And smart! We stole a trick from Dad's deer camp. No matter what we're drinking, there's no fine stemware involved. We're serious about hydration, whether it's water, iced tea, or an adult beverage. Everyone has a big Yeti water bottle with their name on it. We call it an all-terrain drinking vehicle.

But sometimes we'll want a wineglass for something special. Maybe it's something new from our Red 55 Winery, a business I can't believe I get to be in. But why not have a business named after your first pickup? If you're lucky enough to ever have a candy-apple-red step-side, you *should* celebrate it with a winery.

When we're opening a bottle of Crazy Ex-Girlfriend, which is our sweet white, our rich Vice Malbec, the pure-fun Wildcard Moscato, or the drier Kerosene Pinot Grigio, we don't want to spill a drop. So all of our wineglasses—which double as excellent rocks glasses—are stemless. Dad would say, "You don't want doggy tails knocking your good whiskey over."

It's never about how much or how little you drink, but how you drink it. It can sneak up on you, though.

Mom swears Heidi's crackers are dangerous. She literally tells everybody, "Watch out for those crackers! They'll get you drunk! You start eating those and you're gonna get *really* thirsty."

Not that all that's a problem. If you're not driving, if you're having fun, if nobody's gonna get hurt, just make sure you drink plenty of water along the way. And if you don't, there's always the hair-of-the-dog brunch to set you right. Depending on how much time we have to pull it together, Princess V and Mom may have brought all the fixings for a Bloody Mary bar. That's another way to keep it healthy—you can get a bunch of your vegetables in while you're taking the edge off the morning after.

I REMEMBER ONE TRIP TO VICKI'S RIVER HOUSE DOWN AT CADDO IN East Texas where the Little Cypress River flows into the lake. Probably ten of us girls just fifteen minutes from Jefferson. I pulled a 1975 two-toned Argosy camper I called Agnes—all 32 feet of her—all the way from Oklahoma and had to back into the hookup in the yard. Now, we know some people don't think girls are great backer-uppers, but I did it! Got it right straight in—and up to the hookup! We all cheered when I put it in park and opened the door.

To celebrate, we sat around the fire listening to music. I played some Haggard songs. It was a Saturday night, and the neighbors were all out with their golf carts and four-wheelers. For some reason, perhaps the Tito's, I started yelling, "Stranger danger!" out the side door, even though Vicki clearly knew everybody. I kept hollering, "You don't suit our fancy, Nancy!" and "You're at the wrong end of my barrel, Daryl." I just wouldn't stop.

We laughed for hours about embarrassing Vicki in front of the neighbors. Later, I wrote a song with Brent Cobb called "Barrel Daryl," which I've yet to record. It's almost as much fun as that night was, which is pretty much what you're after.

Camping
ZIPLOC OMELETS

MAKES AS MANY INDIVIDUAL OMELETS AS YOU'D LIKE

FOR EACH OMELET

2 large eggs

Pinch each of kosher salt and
freshly ground black pepper

MIX-IN OPTIONS

Chopped bacon

Grated cheese

Chopped sausage

Chopped tomatoes

Chopped bell peppers

Chopped onions

Chopped mushrooms

FOR each omelet, break the eggs into a zip-top bag and season with the
salt and pepper. Add the mix-ins of your choice. Seal the bag and shake
thoroughly to scramble. If desired, use a Sharpie to label the bags with your
name. Place the omelet bag in boiling water for about 15 minutes, until the
eggs are set. Then just roll the omelet out onto a plate.

Rick's
CAMPFIRE CASSEROLE

SERVES 1

Cooking spray

1 medium potato, cut into
1-inch cubes

6 baby carrots

1 small yellow onion,
thinly sliced

⅓ pound ground meat (turkey,
venison, or beef)

½ teaspoon kosher salt

½ teaspoon freshly ground
black pepper

Ketchup or Paw Paw Sauce
(page 53), for serving

OPTIONS

1 small frozen corn on the cob

¼ cup sliced mushrooms

¼ cup cubed or sliced zucchini

LAY out a large piece of heavy-duty aluminum foil or 2 sheets of regular foil (big enough to accommodate your ingredients). Spray the foil with cooking spray.

LAY the potato, carrots, and onion, along with any of the optional ingredients you'd like, down the center of the foil. Crumble the meat over the vegetables and sprinkle with the salt and pepper.

FOLD the foil up, edge to edge, then fold both edges together at the top to seal. Do the same with the ends to make a leakproof packet. Wrap securely with another sheet of foil, if not using heavy-duty foil.

CAMPFIRE COOKING

Prepare a hot fire large enough to cover the number of packets you have prepared.

AFTER the fire has burned down to the coals, shovel the hot coals back, place the packets in the firepit, and shovel the coals back over the packets. (If you have sealed your packets sufficiently, no ashes will make their way into your food.) Cook over the coals for 30 to 35 minutes. (You can also cook these in a 350°F oven or a covered grill for 45 minutes to 1 hour.)

GENTLY brush or rub off any ashes from the packets with a cloth or paper towel. Unfold and enjoy your meal, then crumple up your "plate" and toss it in the trash! We serve ours with plenty of ketchup or Paw Paw Sauce!

Dutch Oven (Coffee Can) CAMPFIRE COBBLER

SERVES 8 TO 10

Cooking spray

1 (29-ounce) can sliced peaches (in heavy syrup)

1 (15.25-ounce) box yellow cake mix

½ cup light brown sugar

1 tablespoon ground cinnamon

4 tablespoons (½ stick) unsalted butter, cut into chunks

IF cooking in the oven, preheat to 350°F.

COVER the inside of a 10- or 12-inch Dutch oven with aluminum foil for easy cleanup. Spray the foil with cooking spray.

POUR the canned peaches into the Dutch oven (juices and all). Pour the cake mix evenly over the peaches—no need to stir. Sprinkle the brown sugar and cinnamon over the mix. Place the chunks of butter evenly on top. Place the lid on the Dutch oven and transfer to a firepit full of hot coals or to the oven. For firepit cooking, cover the lid in hot coals. Cook for 45 minutes. Serve warm with ice cream or cool whip.

Spiced
HOT CRACKERS
"Heidi Crackers"

MAKES TWO GALLON-SIZE ZIP-TOP BAGS OF CRACKERS

1 cup canola oil

2 packets dry buttermilk ranch dressing mix (I like Hidden Valley Ranch)

1 tablespoon red pepper flakes

1 (16-ounce) box saltine crackers (I like Zesta)

TO each of two gallon-size zip-top bags, add ½ cup oil, 1 package dressing mix, and ½ tablespoon red pepper flakes. Seal the bags and shake well so the ingredients are mixed thoroughly. Pour 2 sleeves of crackers into each bag, reseal, and toss to coat the crackers. Continue to toss, turning the bags periodically to distribute the mixture evenly.

STORE the crackers in the sealed bags 'til "served." They should last 6 to 7 days at room temperature.

Jalapeño
PIMENTO CHEESE

SERVES 4 TO 6

2 tablespoons extra-virgin olive oil

1 cup finely chopped yellow onion

1 cup finely chopped red bell pepper

2 cups grated sharp cheddar cheese

½ cup mayonnaise

1 jalapeño, halved, seeded, and finely chopped

IN a skillet over medium-high heat, heat the oil. Add the onion and bell pepper and sauté until softened and the onion is translucent, about 7 minutes. Remove from the heat and set aside to cool.

MEANWHILE, in a bowl, gently fold the cheese and mayo together to incorporate. Add the jalapeño, then fold in the cooled onion mixture.

SERVE on bread or crackers, melt onto tortilla chips in the microwave, mix into omelets, or put in tortillas or on top of hamburgers.

Wanda the Wanderer

AIRSTREAMS, CAMPERS, AND A WHOLE LOT OF LOVE

When I signed my record deal with Sony Nashville, the first thing I bought was a four-wheeler for my brother and me. We grew up surrounded by woods, but we couldn't afford those sorts of things when we were kids. So we raced around on our four-wheelers, having all the fun we thought we'd missed out on.

But the first *real* purchase I made when I became a recording artist was a '52 Flying Cloud. I was twenty-two years old, and that was *my* very own traveling Airstream dream. It was freedom and a space of my own. I could just pack up and go wherever I wanted. When you're doing 250 shows a year as a young artist, not including the other workdays that are part of trying to make it, I can't begin to tell you what that kind of freedom means. Early on, I realized that being on a bus with eleven dudes is what this life is about. I'm not complaining, because I have a great band and crew. But it's a lot, all the time, because you're flying down the road or killing time in a land submarine with all these people you're not related to or in love with.

I remember at one point calling Duane Clark, my longtime business manager and friend, and asking, "Can you please price out some stuff for me? Can you tell me how much a second bus would be? Or how much a few months at a mental health place would cost? Because I am doing one or the other."

You can't cheat doing the work when you're building a career. And you don't want to *not* play for the fans, getting out there and making music. My gypsy heart was so fulfilled by that, by going out and playing all these songs, living the life I'd seen Willie Nelson, Emmylou Harris, and Merle Haggard living when I was growing up. They were always pulling up, playing their shows, then pulling out for somewhere else.

But fulfilled isn't the same as fed! My trailer was that for me. Having my Airstream meant I wasn't at the mercy of a schedule. I didn't have to think about other people's stuff. It was almost like "make your own escape." Flip a coin, which direction are we going?

Ashley Monroe, my longtime BFF, took a trip with me pretty early on. We

went camping at a lake in Oklahoma, which is how the Pistol Annies were born! She told me she'd just written with this girl named Angaleena Presley, who was pretty cool. Ash and I wrote six songs that weekend. When we got back, we met up and wrote with Angaleena, and we realized: together we could write all these songs that weren't gonna work for *any* single one of us, but they were kind of the unspoken part of each of us put together.

Out in the world with your Airstream, you're so free. You can go places you'd never get to in your day-to-day life, let alone on your tour routing. There's no room to drop stuff into the travel schedule. Suddenly, it *is* you and whomever you're traveling with.

Annie—that's my Airstream's name—is a doll. Princess V told us about her. I said to my parents, "Let's go look at it." She was so cute, and the people who were selling cared about that little Airstream so much. It was

in original condition, with homemade curtains and bedding that matched. We're talking sage-green material that matched the couch, and '50s paneled cabinets with sage green on the ceilings. It had two beds, and I knew: this was going to give me everything I wanted. Luke and I had grown up with a pop-up camper, so I loved traveling and sleeping wherever the whim and the road took us. Of course, I'd never really hauled anything like Annie before. Annie's only sixteen feet, so she's pretty small. But it's the first time! I went to see the Airstream with my parents and Princess V. I bought her. My dad helped me hitch her up . . . and away we all went.

I never looked back.

The beauty of Airstreams is all about being halfway: halfway gone because you're on the road, and halfway home because you're pulling your little extra home behind you. You've got somewhere to go, wherever you are, that's yours, and the people who love that kind of easy living find each other.

When the six of us, including my best friend April, who's a next-wave Ya-Ya, are getting ready to meet up—and we meet *up* all over—we have a group text chat, figuring out all the details. Is there anything anyone needs? Are we in a vibe? Some trips you just have a hankering to do, and you should. Whether we're in the woods or by a river, we all load up our coolers and the fridge for three, four days—and we're gone.

And once you get started, you'll find that Airstreams are all so individual and personal that you can't stop. I've also got a '75 Argosy, an Airstream competitor that only lasted for two years before they were absorbed into the company. I rescued the poor thing right off the side of the road. I saw a sign that said, "$1,200 or best offer." I thought, "Well, shoot." I called and asked if it could be hauled. When the answer was yes, I couldn't just leave it. I thought, "Am I crazy for buying this?" But when you're a songwriter, you just know those old girls have stories. You have to be patient sometimes to get 'em out.

I gotta tell you, it took us a bit to get Agnes going. She still had a good frame, so I did a little patch job. My parents knew a guy. We got her painted at an airplane hangar, just a paint job and a little spit shine—and we were able to get her out on the road. But she went through so *many* transformations!

When we started, I can't even tell you. The smell! We had to start there. We got some cheap fabric from Walmart, just to carry us over until we could really get it done. The only thing wrong was that life had taken it out of Agnes more than a little bit.

Agnes had a few tricky little things about her, too, that were pretty cool. There was a shelf that was the size of CDs. When I saw that, I put in a JBL CD player, the first real indulgence, and I robbed the stash of CDs my dad still had from back in the day. Remember those Columbia House Record Club deals, where you buy one and get seven for a penny? There was a bunch of random stuff he still had, but you know what floated our boat the most? K. T. Oslin's *Songs from an Aging Sex Bomb*! It was always on in my mom's car or my Argosy, all the time.

As soon as we got Agnes going, we all convoyed seven and a half hours to South Texas, down to Boerne. We couldn't wait! And that's where Vicki and I joined the Airstream Club. She has a '75 named Tiffany Blue. We decided it was time. They had a whole ceremony for us at a KOA campground with a little pavilion. They literally crowned us! It was so sweet and so perfect to be part of something where people just love traveling, pulling their home behind them. And it's not just about me, Mom, her friends, and my friends, though that's a pretty big part of it. The fact is, in my life, my little Airstreams have given me a space that's mine. No matter where I go, no matter what is going on, I have a space of my own.

I took a page from all the Airstreamers when I hit the road, touring as a young act who *literally* had nowhere to go at the venues. Often you can't get your bus close to the stage or even to the building; the trailers they bring in for

dressing rooms can be drafty, dirty, disgusting—and they have absolutely, 100 percent no vibe. That's where Wanda comes in! I named Wanda the Wanderer after my grandma, who had the most gypsy heart but somehow never really went anywhere. It was my way of letting her see the world. Like my grandmother, Wanda's never met a stranger, likes a strong cocktail, and never loses her tiara!

We were on the festival circuit when it hit me hard that we had nowhere to go. So, I thought, "What if we just have a rolling bar?" I called Amie and Jolie, the Junk Gypsies. They knew about an Airstream shell that would be perfect. The first incarnation of Wanda was "cosmic

cowgirl": sky-blue rockets everywhere, and literally everything and anything that encompasses what you'd think that phrase means. It was fresh and crazy, and I loved it.

When we'd pull her up, you could feel the energy change. Wanda ended up being quite "the thing," the place where I made more friends, starting at Lilith Fair, because people could come together and just be. You never knew who might turn up out there: the Court Yard Hounds, who are Texas girls on the lam from the Chicks; Sarah McLachlan; Kevin Costner one night because he'd come to the show; Brandi Carlile when she was just starting out; Colbie Caillat.

Everyone's band and crew were welcome. Get a drink, c'mon in! It made for quite the mix of people and broke down a lot of barriers, because no matter what kind of music you played or how famous you were, after the shows we had zero expectations. Wanda was a real conversation starter for sure. People were so impressed we had an Airstream strictly for drinking and snacks and hanging out. Sometimes people would look at her a little bewildered, but to have a place like Wanda? They got used to her real fast.

Wanda not only made a lot of friends out of a lot of strangers, but she also even brought some of my heroes to me! Jessi Colter visited with us in Wanda. When we were playing Oklahoma City one year, *the* Wanda Jackson came out to see our show. Afterward, she came over to Wanda. We got to talking, and I learned that her husband's name is Wendell. Well, I have a gutted '68 International Land Yacht, and I'd named him Wendell! I had *no* idea then that it was also Wanda Jackson's husband's name, but it just fit that Land Yacht. We all got to laughing about it—me and an icon who's in the Rock & Roll, Country Music, and Rockabilly Hall of Fames. That's what Wanda the Wanderer does.

Wanda the Airstream (like Wanda Jackson) is a seasoned road warrior. The places she's been, the things she's seen. We used to joke that it's a good thing she can't talk, or we'd all be in trouble. But even more, she's been there for us when we just needed to blow off steam and talk about anything *but* the music business. In an Airstream you feel so at home, it's like you *are* at home—even if you're in the middle of a six-week run and you've been everywhere but the places you've lived.

I know it feels like I'm repeating myself, but Airstreams are something almost more than love. Once you've had the freedom—and gone places you couldn't really travel to any other way—you get addicted. I once booked a festival in Ohio because I knew it was one town over from Jackson Center, Ohio, where the Airstream factory is located. Before we could even call the factory to ask about a tour, they'd heard I was playing and reached out to ask us if I wanted to come see the place. See what I mean about Airstream people?

I may've been more excited about getting to see the place where baby Airstreams are born than they were to meet me. When I went to the factory, they had banners everywhere saying, "Welcome Miranda Lambert!" Those folks have such passion for what they do; those Airstreams are made with pure love and actual manpower. It's truly an old-school assembly line. Humans touch every single part of each Airstream trailer. It takes two people to put in a rivet, and they have 2,800 rivets in the smallest Airstreams. Think about that.

They put every single camper in a rain chamber to make sure it's not going to leak. They also have a heat chamber to put the campers in to make sure they can withstand the heat out on the road, because when you're encased in aluminum, maintaining the proper temperature is critical.

They let me explore each line and each part of the process of building a trailer, and I got to meet all the wonderful people who literally make Airstreams. Just seeing those faces, listening to them tell me about their jobs and how things fit together, it struck me how much goes into building an Airstream—and why they hold their value the way they do. But it's more than that. All the hands-on stories of each Airstream before it even leaves the plant, that's what makes America great. People who care, putting their hearts into something they believe in. They haven't changed how they make 'em that much over the years either, because if it ain't broke . . .

And remember when I said you can't knock off Wanda's crown? I wasn't kidding. Eight years ago, she got run off the road in a snowstorm. She wasn't totaled, but it wasn't good. When they pulled her out of the ditch and were sending her to the shop, one of the wrecker guys laughed and said, "My God! All that, and she didn't lose her crown!"

She is a real queen! So much so, she's even done her *own* tour. When my *Platinum* album was coming out, she hit the road, too, appearing in all these Walmart parking lots. People would show up to get their pictures taken with Wanda! It was wild. To see my fans having as much fun with her as we do? That's what my Airstream love is all about.

7

SINGING FOR MY SUPPER AND CHASING THE DREAM

▼▼▼▼▼▼▼▼▼▼▼▼▼▼▼▼▼▼▼▼▼▼▼▼▼▼▼▼▼▼▼▼▼▼

Home-Cooked Meals and All the Flavors of Texas

When you're seventeen, eighteen years old, you're impressionable. Every single thing you love, you love in a way that sets you on fire. Steve Earle's *I Feel Alright* is one of the records from that time of my life. I decided, along with my family, to get serious about going after my dream of making music and living my life in songs. When I heard that album, it burned a hole straight into me, and I never got over it.

You have to understand, Texas music doesn't work the same way as what you hear on regular country radio does. That's a business, a really big business. There's a way they do things in commercial mainstream country, with a whole system that kicks in once you're signed.

But in Texas, if you have that dream, you can go chase it. You can get up and sing, find a few places that'll let you play even though you're too young to be inside. Make a little record, send it out to bookers, writers, and radio stations—and then hit the road. They call it "chasing the dream" for good reason.

It's pretty simple. Visit radio stations if they'll have you; you'd be surprised by the people who will give a kid a chance. Play shows in the places you've seen other Texas-based artists on their way up, like Jack Ingram, Cooder Graw, or Reckless Kelly. If you've ever seen the movie *Coal Miner's Daughter*, with Sissy Spacek playing Loretta Lynn, you've seen how it works. Get in the car and start driving: it's you against the world. Or, in my case, it's Mom, me, and a cooler full of snacks.

We put my CDs in the back of the truck and hit the road. It was a little self-financed project, with a picture my mom took on the cover; not much by today's standards, but it was 100 percent me at the time.

There's a Texas Music Chart, which focuses on all the artists making music across Texas and Oklahoma. We had a list of all the local radio stations, and I'd call all of them. I literally had my weekly radio "call book," and after a while, some of the on-air disc jockeys expected my call and sometimes would put me on the air. And then there were the DJs who had enough clout to play whatever they wanted. We leaned on those guys real hard.

My mom, who's always been the squeaky wheel, was, like, "We can do this."

She's always had that kind of faith. Considering the way she created the House That Built Me and saw so many people through so many tough times, if she believed, well, I did too.

We chased it! From San Angelo to Amarillo to Lubbock, and Bandera to Boerne to New Braunfels, we drove miles and miles and miles in Mom's Ford Expedition, listening to records by artists we loved—and listening to all those radio stations we were calling to know what they were playing. There were even days when I had an idea for a song; I'd crawl in the back seat with my guitar and try to write. When we'd get to a radio station, Mom would usually stay out in the car. If I got lucky and they actually put me on the air, she wanted to be able to listen. So I'd go in all by myself.

We scrimped to make this journey work, but we did it. I never thought of it as cutting corners. To me, everything we did was part of a mad, crazy adventure. We were out there making things happen—however small—rather than waiting on destiny to come calling. Why take chances, right?

And I have to tell you: we ate great. Probably because my mom thought ahead. We had way better food than anything you could find at truck stops or places along the road. There was always a picnic, packed up and ready to go. She'd have premade breakfast tacos or burritos: sausage, cheese, and eggs all wrapped up. She'd serve them with some fruit, so we got our vitamins. Lunch would be a sandwich, maybe ham and cheese, tuna salad, or bologna on white bread. She just wasn't a junk food kind of mom, so we also always had carrots and celery sticks and an apple too.

I joke now that we had homemade Lunchables long before their time. On "fancy" days we might have deviled eggs, chicken salad sliders, and melon balls. Sometimes Mom would just go all out. All those delicious things would be packed up in a little baggie in our cooler filled with ice. She would stop in a park just to have a few minutes out of the car to get some fresh air, and we would literally have a little picnic. We'd spread everything out, laughing and making up strategies. We were also really grateful to be out there going from station to station.

We didn't stop much, though. The way my mom saw things, if we didn't stop and spend time in a restaurant, we might be able to hit another radio station. When you're rolling like that, five instead of four is a much bigger day. Most of our trips were just two or three days, so we had to make the most of every hour. We'd have our list of stations, maybe even have some appointments. Texas stations back then were a lot looser. Gatekeepers let me talk to the disc jockey or even play on the air—a lot more even than when I was on a major label a few years later.

It's a little bit crazy. My dad was very clear about what we were doing. He said, "We're spending your college money on this CD and for you and your mom to go traipsing all over Texas, so you better be serious." We were. Even when I had pigtails and had to sit outside the bar between sets, I *knew* in my bones I wanted to play music.

Most people don't realize I had a #1 on the Texas chart before I was ever on *Nashville Star*, the talent contest on the USA Network. Mom and I knew what we wanted, and for all we didn't know about what we were doing, we let passion be our guide. We chased that little CD up and down every major and minor highway across Texas, trying to create believers. I can't think of a time, once we got serious about launching my career, when I wasn't going to a show, or listening to music, or out there playing on my own or with a band. It turns out what Mom and I were doing really *was* my college.

This all probably sounds like either some made-up country redneck shit or some kind of Hallmark cowgirl movie, but that's how it was. It was a totally different time, but I think when you want it to happen like I did, nothing will stop you. Even now, I know there are kids out there in Texas and Oklahoma who are chasing the songs and their idea of what country music is down the highway. It's a different way to do it, but it teaches you *how* to do it.

And Mom and I would listen to so many records. We'd get in the truck, pop something in, and turn it up. Sometimes you'd just get gut punched. Those are the records you know you'll *always* know and come back to. Mom and I would be there, sitting in silence; then one of us would say, "What just happened?" and the other would scream, *"Play it again!"*

Emmylou Harris's *Red Dirt Girl* really sticks out to me that way. We were driving through West Texas, and all that horizon was just rolling out in front of us. Those songs poured out of the speakers, and I remember reaching for the little book inside the jewel box case to find the credits.

Realizing that Emmylou had written all those songs? That just hit me. Wherever the songs and characters had come from, I wanted to know Lillian from the song "Red Dirt Girl." I remember thinking, "I *gotta* meet this girl!"

I was on this mission already, but the stakes went up in that moment because I saw how much more all this music, the songs and playing, could mean. I wanted to be doing what Emmylou was doing. Hearing her album, I knew I wanted to make albums that were powerful for people in the same way hers was for me. That feeling of a whole album, the way it builds up inside you and shapes the way you see the world, was life-changing for me.

Music was always as much a part of fun and entertaining at our house as the cheese dip, Heidi's crackers, or the deviled eggs. When your daddy knows how to do a guitar pull and keep everyone singing until morning, everybody wants to be there! You see that and grow up knowing that music—and food—really pull people together.

"Mr. Bojangles" might've been the first song I remember. I got deep early with the Guy Clark stuff, the John Prine songs. But *Red Dirt Girl* could be me. Me, or the me I wanted to be. And Steve Earle's *I Feel Alright* was everything my teenage self was about: untamed, defiant, happy out there on the road. I didn't know how I was going to get there, but I understood from that album, and from Emmylou's, that I was absolutely going to give it my heart to make it happen. The beauty of being so young, barely a teenager, is that your heart may break pretty hard, but you learn you can bounce back pretty fast too.

Sometimes we'd stay in a really cheap motel, then maybe splurge on Chili's if we'd had a tough day. And, of course, we had the Fischer sisters, Heidi and Vicki, to lean on. Anytime we were anywhere near Austin, we'd land at their house. Mom knew the injection of all that love could only be a good thing. Sometimes just being around all that girl power and friendship is like plugging into a generator of the best kind of vibes. Heidi and Vicki might've worked all day—and they worked hard—but when they hit the house, it was a giant grown-up slumber party. These were two of my mother's best friends, so they'd exchange stories about people we all knew and catch up, and we'd turn each other onto music and enjoy the night.

My mom might be my biggest cheerleader, and Neicy was the first grown-up I talked to about music who treated me as an equal, but Heidi and Vicki were right up there. I met them when I was seven. Vicki was living in Dallas; Heidi was living in Austin in their grandparents' house. Vicki worked for a private investigative agency in Dallas that my parents sometime worked cases with, but you'd never know that to look at her. She later became an investigator with the Texas Inspector General's office, working in Austin, and she was good at it.

Vicki would come see us when my parents were in Dallas working, even before there were radio tours. We'd stay at this Marriott Courtyard that had a gazebo. They'd get some friends and some beers, and Dad would play guitar and I would sing. It was so early in the dream, but they made it feel like this desire I had was a little real. Singing for grown-ups who actually listen when you're singing is powerful. It makes you think you have a shot to make your dream happen.

A year or so later, I met Heidi when we were staying at the Holiday Inn at MoPac and Highway 183. You couldn't not love her. She was so bubbly and cheerful. Not long after, she and Vicki just swept us unto their family.

The Fischers' was a place where people cared not just about music but also about *my* music and *my* dream. Even before I made that little *Miranda Lambert* CD, before I was out there playing in the clubs with my mom or dad accompanying me because I wasn't old enough to be there, the Fischers believed in me when I sang. Throughout the whole experience, they wanted to know every detail, hating on anyone who didn't think I was the best thing ever. After a couple days of dust and making happy for strangers, we'd get to their house, and everything was better. They'd have that table set beautifully, make something a little bit fancy, like salmon with dill sauce, and treat me like a great big star.

What wouldn't they do for me? Heidi even got in trouble for calling one of the local radio stations when my second "official" single was out. She was calling so much to request "Bring Me Down," the disc jockey actually busted her and said, "Heidi! Is that you?"

When I got a little older and my parents let me travel on my own, I would still stay with Heidi and Vicki. They listened to every story, heard me talk about every person who was nice or kinda strange, like it was the most interesting thing in the world. When the Dixie Chicks played Austin, Heidi, Vicki, and I all went to the concert together. That was another one of those moments when I could see my whole life in front of me: the great playing, the songs, the throwing your heart out into the world through your music. Heidi and Vicki understood and never told me not to get my hopes up. They believed I'd be onstage too.

No matter what was on my mind, they'd listen. They'd take out some homemade salsa or Heidi's criminally delicious pimento cheese, maybe even a cheese ball, with hot Heidi Crackers at the ready. They'd grab us something to drink and let me tell them *everything*.

It's funny how easy it is to forget the power of a home-cooked meal. When you're out there really pressing to make something happen, nothing feels more "Yes, you can" when you're dead tired than a forkful of a dish you know by heart. Even if it's just something simmering in a slow cooker all day, when you hit the door and get that scent of home-cooked dinner, you know somebody cared enough to think ahead and wanted to feed you a nurturing meal after whatever you'd been though.

But Heidi and Vicki? They knew how to feed a dream. To a couple wanderers, like my mom and me, it felt like home. When you'd wake up at their house, there'd be migas or a breakfast casserole waiting. Sometimes

Heidi would make her famous lemon-blueberry muffins. It was heaven, first thing in the morning. And sometimes they'd break out the enchiladas, serving up Texas comfort food like only a Texan can. You can't imagine how soul-filling most of the dishes in this cookbook are! That is part of why I wanted to *do* this, so people everywhere across the country could experience the warm hug that is a plate of the Fischer sisters' enchilada casserole.

Traveling around the world, there's nothing I love more than true Tex-Mex or Neicy's Cajun dishes. To me, that's the flavor of home.

"What's Tex-Mex?"

I get asked that question *all* the time. It's actually inspired endless discussions. In some ways, it depends on where you are and who you're asking. Texans like to go their own way. It's part of the beauty that allows for Dallas to be so different from Austin, and for Houston to be not very much like South Padre Island, and for a million little towns across the state to all have their own personality.

When I was growing up, Tex-Mex was all about the glory of enchiladas, migas, tamales, queso or cheese dip, chili, even taco soup. I'm not sure if Neicy's jalapeño-sausage corn muffins count, but they should! It's stuff you can grab and go, or food you can linger over with your friends, talking about Flaco Jiménez and the Texas Tornados or Willie Nelson while enjoying every single bite. But it's bigger than that too.

One of the things about Tex-Mex is that it merges two worlds, two cultures. South Texas, the Rio Grande Valley, El Paso, San Antonio, and Northern Mexico shared pieces of their cuisines a bit, borrowing from one another to make something special. Because there was so much ranching in Texas, grilled beef and chili con carne became a part of it, as did chili powder and cumin.

In 1968, the *Los Angeles Times* wrote a story trying to unpack the food that was inspired by the Tejanos, the same hybrid local cuisine that probably sparked the legendary Texas songwriter Guy Clark's iconic homage to "Texas Cookin'." When the *Times* wrote, "if the dish is a combination of Old World cooking, hush-my-mouth Southern cuisine and Tex-Mex, it's from the Texas Hill Country," they nailed it.

That Southern cooking touch, something my mom and all her friends excel at, is part of what makes Tex-Mex so good. They don't scrimp on the cheese. They're not afraid to let things simmer so the flavors really spread out and merge. *And* there's enough spice to grab your tongue with a spark. It's down-home with a little kick. And that is what I think of when I think of home: fresh salsa, jalapeños on the table, Ro-Tel tomatoes, green chiles.

When you have a forkful of homemade enchilada casserole—whether cheese, chicken, beef, or sausage—it's heaven. It is South Texas comfort food that rivals mac 'n' cheese. That's what I was brought up on, so to me, both are gooey, cheesy deliciousness with different carbs. But I'm going to want the enchiladas.

Even something as simple as Heidi's sausage, poblano, and egg tacos: they're grab 'n' go, no big fuss, just easy, healthy, and so flavorful. Maybe that's part of it too. Every single thing that falls into Tex-Mex isn't just tasty, but there are also all kinds of spices, textures, and tastes, so it's never just a chunk of something on a plate or meat between two slices of bread.

There's jalapeño cornbread alone! Even without Neicy's special Mexican sausage corn muffins, you've got cornmeal, cheddar cheese, an onion, creamed corn, and jalapeños taking basic breakfast to a whole other galaxy. With chili, a plate of beans, or big bowl of soup, you've got something genuinely tasty that can stand up to whatever you serve it with. Now that's quite a trick.

Neicy, beyond being the special adult who talked music with a kid as if I was a grown-up, is a full-on Louisianan.

There's a real soul to Neicy, something so quiet you could miss it. But the time she puts into whatever she does, whether making a roux or talking about Delbert McClinton and the way he sings a song, makes whatever she's doing meaningful.

Long before people were watching Paul Prudhomme going "gaaaaah-RON-teeeee!" on television, we had Neicy in our kitchen making honest-to-goodness Cajun magic! All that flavor, all that spice—she understood how it all worked together. We didn't need to know how she did it. We just wanted more.

Texas and Louisiana border each other. Back when, if you lived in a dry county in Texas, you might run over the state line to get something a little harder to drink than milk. So, for us, the idea of Cajun was a lot like Mexican food. It was something people who lived near us ate. It was never a matter of being authentic or trendy, it was just Neicy.

Everyone has their tricks, and Neicy's extended far beyond Louisiana classics. She brought the essence of who she was into our house with gumbos, jambalayas, étouffées, shrimp 'n' grits. Her jambalaya will make you speak in tongues after the first bite. My mom marvels that Neicy has the patience to wait out a roux and just keep stirring.

What's interesting to me now, and not something I ever thought about when they were putting gumbo over rice for us kids, is the way that Cajun food grew out of French cooking, the same way Tex-Mex came out of Mexico. Cajun is also the perfect counterpoint to Tex-Mex because the flavors—while bursting on your tongue—are so different. Beyond using garlic and green onions, Cajun is about paprika, thyme, red pepper, black pepper, and something called "filé," which you say "FEE-lay." If you know the Hank Williams song "Jambalaya (on the Bayou)," when he or Emmylou Harris sing about life down on the bayou and they get to the line about food that includes crawfish pie and filé gumbo, that's what they're referring to.

I don't know if you can find filé in most grocery stores, but you can get it online. It's crazy: filé is made from ground sassafras leaves. Talk about an unexpected ingredient.

Seasoning may be important, but Neicy will tell you that Cajun food really comes down to the roux and "the holy trinity": finely diced green peppers, onions, and celery that you slow cook to create the body of just about every dish except bread pudding. It's time consuming, getting the dice right, but what's really tricky is the roux. It's the secret weapon in Cajun cooking. It takes the patience of a man when the fish ain't biting, and the will to stir even when it seems like nothing's happening.

When Brendan and I got married, he'd never had Cajun food. He'd grown up in New York and had eaten all over the city, trying every single kind of cuisine imaginable, but somehow he'd never run into Cajun food.

The Dominican in him loves spicy, so when he got his first taste of Neicy's gumbo, he loved it! He ate that bowl of slow-cooked Cajun goodness like a puppy and went back for another bowl—and another the next day. Talk about making the cook happy.

All these women cook not just to feed you but also to make the people at their table smile. Neicy and her brother Zack, who's quite the cook too, have no problem putting in the time to make their home cooking extra special. We all accepted that we'd never make Cajun food like they do because we were never going to put in the time. Neicy will stir, and stir, and stir, and stir, and stir, and then tell you, "It wasn't anything." But it sure is. So *know* this: you have to be patient with it.

Sounds simple, until you have to do it. Believe me.

Get your whisk and keep stirring as the flour starts to slowly turn brown. That brown is what adds the richness and the flavor, but if you don't pay attention, it'll burn. If that happens, you either have to throw it all out and get takeout or start over.

You'd think once that's done, it's simple. Nope, that's just the beginning. You have to slowly—bit by bit—add a coldish liquid, then work it in. Every time you add more water, pan juices, milk, or what have you, you have to keep stirring so the roux doesn't get lumpy or lose its consistency. Then, when it looks and feels like paste and you think you've ruined it, don't panic! When the roux goes south that way, just exhale and add some more liquid; inhale and keep stirring.

Sounds like a lot of hassle, and for what? Until you've had home-cooked gumbo, you can't understand. It's like the richest stock you've ever tasted, but then it's packed with andouille sausage, okra, bits of chicken sometimes, shrimp or prawns, tomatoes, all the vegetables from the trinity. It cooks slowly and makes the whole house smell like heaven. When you're scooping it out of the pot into a fluffy bowl of rice, you almost have tears in your eyes for how good you know it's going to taste—just mmmmm! Ladle it over everything, grab a piece of cornbread, and get ready to be changed for life.

Being blessed to have Neicy in my life meant that this was another taste along my journey. How lucky am I? Neicy is a woman who, even if it's just four or five people for dinner, is going to roll in with no less than four gallons of whatever she's bringing. She'll say it doesn't taste as good if you're cutting the recipe in half, but she'll also have a freezer-proof plastic bag with your name on it. She knows you're going to want another meal, and in this crew's fashion, she's happy to oblige.

Brendan, my husband, got so obsessed with her magic, he literally stood at her elbow enough times to truly learn the process and techniques for making roux and the rest of the Cajun specialties. He's gotten to where he pretty much nails it, but he still texts Neicy or Zack pictures, asking, "Is this the right color?" He'll wait for the reply. Sometimes it's, "Yes, it's perfect." Other times it's, "I think it needs five more minutes." If Neicy and I have our secret language of music, Brendan, Neicy, and her brother are glued together through the subtleties of roux and the other Cajun mysteries.

Those ladies, who were old enough to be my mother, all treated me like an equal. They looked out for me, knew how young I was, but still made me feel like I was one of them. It was the greatest sorority I could ever be a part of because it's life and not just a club.

Over the years, I've sung at their weddings and events, and these women always came out to the shows anytime we were close enough. When I was sixteen and seventeen, they'd come out and party because they knew they had a designated driver—me! I'm so lucky I had these women in my life. They taught me how to be strong, how to build a community and a family, and how to enjoy laughter through food and music.

When I was a kid, I wasn't thinking about what we were eating or where we were going. If somebody wanted me to take out my guitar and sing, nothing made me happier. *That* was the point of what my mom and I were doing, plain and simple.

Looking back, I realize it wasn't that I didn't care what we ate. My mom and her circle of friends made sure we had so much wholesome, delicious food no matter where we landed. I was hungry, voraciously hungry I now realize; but I was hungry to make it happen—not for the next meal but for my future.

Sun-Dried Tomato
CHEESE BALL

SERVES 10 TO 12

8 ounces cream cheese

2 cups grated sharp cheddar cheese

¼ cup chopped oil-packed sun-dried tomatoes

¼ cup chopped green onion

¼ cup chopped black olives

½ teaspoon garlic salt

½ cup chopped pecans

IN a bowl, mix together the cream cheese, cheddar, sun-dried tomatoes, green onion, olives, and garlic salt. Form into a ball. Cover and refrigerate overnight.

PUT the pecans on a plate. Roll the cheese ball in the pecans until fully coated before serving.

Migas

SERVES 4 TO 6

6 large eggs

¼ cup whole milk

1 teaspoon kosher salt

¼ teaspoon freshly ground black pepper

1 (10-ounce) can diced tomatoes with green chiles, drained (I like Ro-Tel)

6 corn tortillas, cut or torn into strips

½ pound breakfast sausage or venison sausage

1 cup grated American cheese

Salsa, sliced avocado, cilantro, or other garnishes (optional)

IN a large bowl, whisk together the eggs, milk, salt, and pepper. Add the tomatoes and tortilla strips. Let soak for 20 minutes.

COOK the sausage in an electric skillet on medium-high for 8 to 10 minutes, draining off any excess grease. Add the egg mixture and cook, stirring occasionally, until the eggs are set. Top evenly with the American cheese. Turn off the skillet and let sit until the cheese melts.

TO serve, roll up in a flour tortilla with salsa, avocado slices, cilantro, or other garnishes, as desired.

Sausage
CORNBREAD MUFFINS

MAKES 2 DOZEN MUFFINS

Cooking spray

2 large eggs

⅔ cup whole milk

2 (8.5-ounce) packages corn muffin mix (I like Jiffy)

1 pound crumbled cooked hot pork sausage

1 (15-ounce) can whole kernel corn, drained

1 (4-ounce) can diced green chiles

2 cups grated cheddar cheese

PREHEAT the oven to 400°F. Grease 24 muffin cups with cooking spray or use paper liners.

IN a large bowl, beat the eggs and milk together until well combined. Add the muffin mix and stir until just moistened. Stir in the sausage, corn, green chiles, and cheese to combine.

FILL the prepared muffin cups two-thirds full. Bake for 25 minutes, until light golden-brown.

Stacked
ENCHILADA BAKE

SERVES 6 TO 8

Cooking spray

2 tablespoons vegetable oil

1½ pounds ground beef

1 medium yellow onion, chopped

1 (10-ounce) can red enchilada sauce

2 teaspoons ground cumin

2 teaspoons paprika

1 teaspoon kosher salt

½ teaspoon freshly ground black pepper

12 (6-inch) corn tortillas, cut in half

1 (16-ounce) jar salsa verde

3 cups grated cheddar cheese

¼ cup chopped fresh cilantro

Sliced avocado, for garnish (optional)

PREHEAT the oven to 350°F. Lightly grease a 9 x 13-inch baking dish with cooking spray.

IN a skillet over medium-high heat, heat the oil. Add the ground beef and onion and brown for 5 to 7 minutes. Drain off the fat. Stir in the enchilada sauce, cumin, paprika, salt, and pepper, then reduce the heat to medium. Cook for 20 minutes.

LAYER half of the tortillas in the prepared baking dish, overlapping them slightly. Top with half of the beef mixture, half of the salsa verde, and half of the grated cheese. Repeat with the remaining tortillas, beef mixture, and salsa verde, and top evenly with the remaining cheese. Sprinkle with the chopped cilantro.

BAKE, uncovered, for 30 to 35 minutes, until hot and bubbly. Garnish with avocado, if desired.

Neicy's GUMBO

SERVES 8

1 cup vegetable oil

1 cup all-purpose flour

1½ cups chopped yellow onion

1 cup chopped celery

1 cup chopped bell pepper

1 pound smoked sausage, cut into ½-inch pieces

1½ teaspoons kosher salt

¼ teaspoon cayenne

3 bay leaves

6 cups chicken stock

1 pound boneless chicken meat, cut into 1-inch chunks (see Cook's Note)

1 tablespoon Creole seasoning (I like Tony Chachere's)

Rice, for serving

ADD the oil and flour to a large Dutch oven over medium heat, whisking slowly and constantly for 20 to 25 minutes to make a dark roux. (It should be a milk chocolate color.)

ADD the onion, celery, and bell pepper to the pot and continue stirring until the vegetables are softened, 5 to 7 minutes. Add the sausage, salt, cayenne, and bay leaves. Continue cooking and stirring for 3 or 4 minutes. Stir in the chicken stock, increase the heat to high, and bring to a boil. Reduce the heat to medium-low and let cook for an hour, stirring occasionally, until slightly thickened and the flavors have melded.

MEANWHILE, sprinkle the chicken chunks with the Creole seasoning and stir to coat. Add the seasoned chicken to the pot and allow to simmer for an additional hour, occasionally skimming off the fat that rises to the surface.

REMOVE the bay leaves before serving. Serve the gumbo over rice.

COOK'S NOTE *You can use rotisserie chicken instead of raw chicken. Just pull the meat off the bone and add to the pot according to the steps on the opposite page. Instead of seasoning the chicken, add the Creole seasoning to the pot (reduce to 1 teaspoon). You can also add 1 teaspoon of filé powder before serving to thicken the gumbo.*

8

DINNER WITH THE GOOD CHINA

▼▼▼▼▼▼▼▼▼▼▼▼▼▼▼▼▼▼▼

"I don't want to <u>have</u> to use my pretty stuff;
I want to use my pretty things <u>all the time</u>."

I'm blessed. Between Mom and Nonny, I learned about the magic of a pretty table. Here's the secret: it doesn't take much.

At our house, *nothing* ever went to the table in the jar, box, or bottle it came in. You found a small bowl, a little plate, a tray. It wasn't always fancy, but it made such a difference in how you felt when you sat down to eat.

What's funny, too, is that as different as mothers and daughters can be, that's one thing Mom and Nonny had in common. They made sure when something went on the table, it was presented with love.

Nonny was always more formal than my mom. She had her daily dishes, of course. They had geese with ribbons around their necks, and the border had ducks and geese cut out on them. She had a second set in hunter green and red. The dinner plates had a rooster stamped right in the middle; the salad plates had a matching checked gingham border.

Nonny had big kitchen style. She had a little island where she and Pop-Pop ate standing up sometimes. Those walls had a full-on wooden border with carved hearts, horses and carriages, and roosters. I remember, when I was ten, saying to Mom, "We have to tell Nonny she needs a new border." My mom just laughed and said, "You tell her!"

That border is *still* there.

WHEN I WAS GROWING UP, NONNY HAD HER WATERFORD CRYSTAL AND her good china in an old-school china cabinet in the dining room. While she had everyday stuff, she never used the basics on us, even little sausages or a cheese ball she served on a crystal platter with little bitty paper napkins.

My mom, who lands on the spectrum between china hoarder and dish-aholic, serves the same way. Whether it's frozen pizza or made from scratch, love means properly setting the table, everything served on a proper serving dish. It might've been hand-me-down, but it brought the table real style.

Some of it *was* hand-me-down stuff. She had her grandmother's china, pieces of Nonny's, even some of my dad's mom's things. It was total mix and match, a little all over the place, but it worked. Maybe it worked because we knew *all* the love that every one of those plates had been set with, or maybe we just liked all that color.

Colors hold as much memory as the actual pieces in a lot of cases. My mom's most treasured piece of china is probably my great grandmother Lucy Miranda's sea foam–green deviled egg platter. It's so heavy, I swear as kids we thought it was indestructible. When her grandmother passed away, Mom says, it wasn't even "left" to her, just that "everybody knows Beverly makes the deviled eggs," so it went straight to her without question.

I grew up with that light green dish—four generations old—always around. Knowing it was Mom's Grandma's made it feel like an extension of our family. When you grabbed a deviled egg, you'd smile and think about all the fingers from our family that had touched that very same dish.

MOM'S DISHES—HER FANCY SET—HAD A GREEN RIM, WITH PINK FLOWERS tied up like a little bouquet. It went with her French country kitchen, which she'd done up with sponges, paint, and a little determination. The dishes are actually English, made by Royal Doulton. The pattern is called Old Leeds Spray, and they don't make it anymore. If you look online, it says "1912–1956," so that pattern was already long retired by the time those plates and bowls were sitting on our dinner table.

My mom and grandma and their tableware started me on my own Alice in Wonderland adventure. That fanciful having-a-mad-tea-party way of setting a table holds so many possibilities. I love old dishes, because when you touch them you think about all the conversations that were held over those different pieces and whose hands might have held them, washed them, had supper on them, or put them away. More than history, it's love. Or passion. Or growing up. Every set of china holds so many different pieces of somebody's story—not that we'd ever forget Nonny or Mom's grandmother, but this keeps them, somehow, a little bit alive.

It's like a party-within-a-party right there on the table. You look down, with all those different patterns, different eras, different stories swirling together, and you realize how many lives have converged, how far your people have reached. You can even add something as simple as flowers in a mason jar or a bowl of lemons or limes to create an easy centerpiece.

Even more importantly, when you've got a jumble of different pieces, it takes the pressure off. Sometimes when I go to a really fancy dinner and everything looks and feels so expensive, I get nervous. If you're like me, you're probably afraid that if you knock over a glass, you may have broken something old and expensive that can't be replaced.

WHEN I OWNED MY LADYSMITH BED & BREAKFAST, I WANTED THAT sense that so many others had shared these plates. We served a lot of breakfasts in little cast-iron skillets and bakers, but *all* of the dishes were funky and mismatched. We discovered them in little out-of-the-way antique stores, a few junk shops, on Etsy and eBay, and even at yard sales. It seemed like there were a bunch of little stores in Oregon, of all places. You just never know when or where you might run up on something.

If you're feeding anywhere from sixteen to twenty people most mornings, of course you could make it all the same. Matchy-matchy always works, and it's actually pretty easy to do. Buy all the same heavy white china that looks clean and crisp. Lots of people do it, and they say it takes on the atmosphere you're using it in: refined, classic, just so.

But that's sure not the Lambert way! No, ma'am. We mixed it all up, gave people something to talk about. You'd be amazed at the way the guests talked about the different patterns, how they remembered someone they knew who had "dishes just like this," or even talked about some other china pattern that had nothing to do with anything on the table where they were sitting. It seemed to open up windows in their mind and took them back to other places!

"Honor the place" is a good place to start. Since the Ladysmith building was built in 1901, we didn't want all brand new. I wanted things that honored that time but also thrilled the people who were sitting at the table now. For that, bringing in the mee-maw patterns on bowls, plates, teacups, and mugs was about merging the turn of the century with my own eclectic cowgirl/hippie/bohemian shabby-chic rock-and-roll reality.

That aesthetic idea of mixing up all the pieces of who you are carried over to Wanda June, the housewares line I created. I wanted there to be pieces of the women who shaped me reflected in what we are creating for other people's homes.

A lot of the patterns on the dishes come from Nonny's blouses. I went through some of my favorite things of hers, then tried to figure out how to adapt them. Nonny knew how to catch attention. She'd roll out, and people would look. The year she was my date to the Academy of Country Music Awards, they asked her what she was wearing on the red carpet; she told them Dillard's. How sweet—and perfect—is that?

That's why I picked the name Wanda June. I used Nonny to inspire the entire collection of tableware and take-it-on-the-go kitchen things. She loved people, so this is my way of letting her help make it easy for them to get their table started.

Even the coffee mugs, which stack for easy carrying, don't match. Same family of colors, same ideas, but if you break one or go to someone's house with your coffee and leave it behind, no big deal. Next year, there'll be more—and they will complement what you already have.

To me, invoking the people you love in how you live is a great way of touching their love and sharing their energy with others. For this, I wanted to give people a double dose: June is my mom's middle name and, obviously, Wanda is my nonny.

It's always where you are and who you are at the core that matters. And those things you share from the past can help shape your future.

When Nonny died, I got some of the Waterford crystal, as well as some of her carnival glass goblets. I took all that stuff to my farm, which is where I have a lot of people come when we're entertaining. The juxtaposing of my little cabin with this special stuff is what I'm talking about. Grill up some chicken and sausage or pull out a bowl of chicken salad, maybe some charcuterie—it becomes an even more special moment when you serve it on crystal.

I want this book to be permission to live and have fun, to enjoy everything in your life. Take all the expectation out of the air before you even get started; just drop the pressure to be perfect. Even if the preacher is coming over, let all that go. Sometimes I think the preacher'd have more fun, too, if people weren't so uptight and nervous, trying to show him how perfect they are.

If the idea is not to judge, then start with yourself. Get down the good china that you never use. Grab the crystal goblets—the ones that if you wet your finger and run it around the rim will "sing" in the wildest tones—and maybe drink your sweet tea or pink wine out of it. If you're not using it, what's the point? And who're you trying to impress?!

The Loaf

A.K.A. "THE ONE THING THAT'LL GET THE RING!"

When I was growing up, my mom's meatloaf was legendary. We had it on birthdays because it was so delicious. We had friends come over on *their* birthdays because they wanted the Loaf too.

A lot of people think of meatloaf as this gray, dry proposition, or something drowned in brown gravy that doesn't taste like much of anything. It's one of those school-lunch deals we've all had and never care if we eat again. *That* was not the Loaf. Not only is it the product of an actual three-part process—the meatloaf, the topping, and the gravy—but it also has all these secret things that make it taste like nothing you've ever had before. Plus, there are all the things going on when you taste it. There's sweetness to it. The meat has so much flavor; it's a little tangy. Then, the topping becomes almost this caramelized layer that makes the Loaf wicked juicy. Anyone who's ever had it is going to want it again. Maybe it's the breakfast sausage/ground beef mixture, or the brown sugar, or the green peppers and onions all

chopped up. And the gravy—made with the juices from the meat, a few tablespoons of the leftover topping, a cup of water, and a lot of pepper and some salt—is literally the color of a pumpkin! You see it and wonder, then you ladle it on and have to repent it's so delicious. It's why when people think of my mom, they think of chicken salad, deviled eggs, and . . . the Loaf.

Early in my career, my publicist was asked for a recipe for a feature *Southern Living* magazine does. Obviously, there was only one classic Bev Lambert to give them: the Loaf. The magazine's concept was simple: her way and my (cough) healthier way. Looking for home-cooking comfort food for their February 2010 issue, they believed they were going to come up with a way to make it—I don't even know the word—close? Because the Loaf is perfection. Absolute, total perfection.

I remember the editors at the magazine were frustrated. They'd had several people make it and thought the recipe needed a few changes. They kept calling and saying their test kitchen couldn't make it work, because they needed to guarantee that the people who try these recipes in their own homes will have them turn out great. All the Ya-Yas just know how much of everything to put in; nobody's ever using a cookbook or a measuring cup or spoon. Mom's measurements were more a clump of brown sugar, a squirt of Worcestershire, or a spoonful of mustard. The magazine's staff couldn't get behind Mom's "use half a sleeve of crackers," so they ended up with "use 32 saltine crackers." I'm not sure now, but that's what they finally decided they could replicate. And once they did, people all over the world started making my mom's already plenty famous meatloaf.

It sounds funny to say that, but, literally, every week people come up to tell me they've made it and how much everyone who's had it loves it. People tell Mom *all* the time—folks she'll meet traveling, who either clipped the recipe out of the magazine when it ran or had someone give it to them, or,

much later, just went looking for it on the internet. You can actually google my mom's Loaf.

And it doesn't matter who you are, the real deal about this meatloaf is this: it *will* get you married.

If you're ready to get that ring— and my mom is gonna ask, "Are you ready?" before she talks you through it—this is *exactly* the meal you cook!

I've done it, *twice*! Heidi's done it. My best friend April's done it. It really works.

When my friend Ashley Monroe (who people know from the Pistol Annies as Hippie Annie) made up her mind about her now husband, John Danks, who was playing baseball for the Chicago White Sox at the time, you can bet she called Lindale, Texas. My mom told Ashley step-by-step on the phone every last single bit of what she needed to do to create the exact Loaf: each ingredient, how to mix it, where to put the pan in the oven. Wasn't too much later that Mom got the call—Ashley was engaged.

My mom thinks the Loaf works because this recipe really feels like home. Because when you put that first forkful in your mouth, it tastes so comforting and really feels satisfying to a man's taste buds and appetite. It never fails. Sometimes I think a week doesn't go by without some girl—but men have made it too—looking to lock down a partner, and *that's* when they get serious about the Loaf. Heck, my brother, Luke, who's been a vegetarian for years, even figured out how to make a vegan Loaf with Impossible "meat" and vegetarian Worcestershire sauce (it doesn't have any anchovies)—and it's delicious too. It doesn't sound right, but when you follow the recipe, even my dad said, "Well, that's pretty good." Luke did make the original version for his boyfriend (now husband) before they became vegetarians.

For a while, my mom made Mini Loafs, enough for maybe a couple

people for a single meal. She'd have a few of them all in the oven, bubbling up under that sweet, savory, almost-beyond-words glaze. She would send them to folks for a little meal when they were coming back to town or caring for a sick relative; she would occasionally freeze one.

But her best way of making the Loaf smaller was her Muffin Loafs. Sometimes, when she entertains, she will actually take little mini-muffin tins, put a tiny cupcake paper liner in the holes, and fill each one up just like it's a regular Loaf. When they come out, piping hot and delicious, she puts a little dollop of mashed potatoes on top. Just like people put whipped cream on their desserts, she uses her creamy mashed potatoes like frosting on a cupcake. People gobble those up in three little bites or two big chomps. It's a lot of work for heavy hors d'oeuvres, but when you see the way people start moaning and hovering over the platters, you smile to yourself because you know: the Loaf is invincible.

The Loaf also brings families together. It's the first thing I made for my husband Brendan's family. Then,

when we decided it was time for our families to all meet—after Brendan and I had gotten married at my farm—it was Mother's Day. I told Mom and Dad, "Why don't you come up and meet Brendan's family? No gun talk, no politics, but I'll make the Loaf."

We introduced the Staten Islanders to the Loaf, which is like their chicken Parm. We were late getting there because of travel delays, and I think Brandon and I were both nervous, but we shouldn't have been. When we walked in the door, everyone was all liquored up, having a big time, and laughing about family stories on both sides. It was awesome.

And my mom, bless her heart, was staying at the impossibly hip SoHo Grand Hotel in lower Manhattan. She knew what the mission was, and she got out there, found a grocery store, and bought all the fixings. Travel delay or no, we were ready to go! And we went for it. That's the thing: whether there's a marriage or a death, you can always count on the fact that there will be a pot or a casserole dish involved, but when it's something you're building to last, it's *always* the Loaf.

The Loaf
BEV'S FAMOUS MEATLOAF

SERVES 6 TO 8

2 pounds lean ground beef

1 pound ground pork sausage

18 saltine crackers, crushed

½ green bell pepper, chopped

½ yellow onion, finely chopped

2 large eggs, lightly beaten

1 tablespoon Worcestershire sauce

1 teaspoon mustard

½ cup firmly packed light brown sugar

½ cup ketchup

2 tablespoons flour

Kosher salt and freshly ground black pepper

PREHEAT the oven to 350°F. Use an 11 x 7-inch baking dish.

ADD the ground beef, sausage, crackers, bell pepper, onion, eggs, Worcestershire, mustard, and ¼ cup of the brown sugar to a medium bowl. Mix with your hands until blended. Shape the mixture into a 10 x 5-inch loaf and place in the baking dish.

BAKE for 1 hour. Remove from the oven; drain the juices into a separate bowl and reserve for the gravy. In a bowl, stir together the ketchup and the remaining ¼ cup brown sugar for the glaze. Reserve 2 to 3 tablespoons of the glaze for the gravy. Spread the rest over the meatloaf. Bake for 15 minutes more, until an instant-read thermometer inserted into the thickest portion registers 160°F. Pour the drained meat juices into a saucepan and heat until hot. Add the flour and stir until thickened. Mix 1½ cups of hot water into the reserved glaze and add it to the saucepan. Cook until it starts to bubble. Remove from the heat and generously season with salt and pepper.

REMOVE the loaf from the oven and let stand for 20 minutes. Then serve directly from the casserole dish, alongside your favorite mashed potatoes topped with the gravy.

9

HOLIDAYS IN THE BITCHIN' KITCHEN

▼▼▼▼▼▼▼▼▼▼▼▼▼▼▼▼▼▼▼▼▼▼▼▼▼▼▼

By now, you know this about my mom, her friends, our family, and everyone else we sweep up into our gypsy, free-spirit, cowgirl world: we love to get together. Any excuse, any reason, any anything—why not? Life is sweeter when you live it with friends, talking about whatever strikes your fancy, mood, or "you won't believe this!" yelp. No matter what was going on, good times or bad, Mama, Vicki, Denise, and Heidi knew how to make everything sparkle, taste good, and fun.

But some things are just for family. My mother was adamant that the holidays are family time. My nonny, mom, and dad *all* took the prize when it came to holidays. We're talking "HOLIDAYS." Definitely all in capital letters, probably with the quotation marks too. Every single holiday was something else—and something special.

I'm not sure who took them the most seriously. Every single adult in my life was so sentimental; they were all obsessed with how to make the most out of each and every moment. Each of them made sure that every holiday was something we'd treasure and remember forever. Besides music—because there was always music—there were always special sit-down meals with fancy little touches and traditions we kept from year to year.

Because my parents worked so hard building a business, as well as bringing people into our house to live with us when they needed help, we were always very grateful at the holidays. Even at Halloween, when we were dressing up and getting tricky, we knew we could celebrate to the max in pure, unadulterated Lambert family style. Sometimes I think The Pink Pistol grew out of that love of the holidays. Mom and her friends just love all the tchotchkes and trinkets, the wreaths and candy dishes, all the ways to set a table and make a house look like whatever holiday it is just exploded everywhere. The Santa this, the reindeer that, the turkey gravy boats, the howling witches and bunny plates. That's what I love about how I was raised. There was no detail too small, no notion too big, that Mom or Nonny couldn't figure out a way to bring to life.

The big battle in our house for years was Nonny versus my mother. In one corner, you had Nonny, the queen of all, who never even filled a gas tank, who wanted exactly the same decorations and meal year after year; in the other corner, you had my mom, the über-babe, who was always into the hottest trend, wanting to change things up and try something different just to keep it interesting.

Those two could dig in like nobody's business, but, of course, Nonny *always* won. We always had the turkey and her dressing, the same casseroles and vegetables. It was always at her house, decorated with the same swag and ornaments. She had to have those old-school things to make sure the traditions endured. Tell you the truth, it was a bit like the chorus of "Automatic," a song I wrote with my friends Nicolle Galyon and Natalie Hemby about how life used to be when it felt like the world moved slower.

It's only worth as much as the time put in
It all just seemed so good the way we had it
Back before everything became automatic

It's funny when you realize some of the real joy of holidays is the anticipation leading up to the event. Knowing that Thanksgiving was coming and that we were going to all be together to count our blessings, eat too much, watch football, maybe sing John Prine, Robert Earl Keen, or George Strait songs while my daddy played guitar—that was almost as much fun as the actual day.

Obviously, Christmas is the Super Bowl of holidays when you're a kid. Thank God my parents are both big kids at heart and got the biggest kick out of everything Christmasy: pageants, parties, Santa, decorating, caroling, and, of course, the presents! But don't think Easter or Halloween, New Year's Eve, July Fourth, or birthdays were any less special, because they weren't. For us, they were all important, all a chance to make memories. Maybe that was because my parents were rebuilding a business during my childhood, after hitting a slow streak in the PI business during the recession of the early '90s. Maybe when you come through that, you count your blessings and celebrate life as often as you can.

All I knew as a little girl—and what I still believe today—was that everyone in our world believed you worked hard, worked full-time, and wanted to make as many wonderful memories as you could. The holidays were sure a great place to start. The joy we felt wasn't earned so much as it was the payoff for everything we put into living our lives right.

So, here is your field guide to the holidays, Lambert-style.

THANKSGIVING

In a word, Thanksgiving at our house was *traditional*. Nonny wouldn't have it any other way. Even after my grandmother was gone, oh, the trauma and the drama we endured trying to get the dressing even close to hers.

I remember once, when we were young, she had pulled the giblets out of the bird. She said to me, "This is the heart," and I was just too scared to touch it. She told me she didn't have the nerve to cook with it either. And that's where the line on my album *The Weight of These Wings* comes from; when I sing "I don't have the nerve to use my heart" in "Use My Heart," it literally comes from making dressing with Nonny all those years ago.

Funny what sticks with you, and how you use it. Sometimes it's just dressing, and sometimes it's something so much more.

Luke and I both tried and tried to get the dressing right, but it just wasn't the same. Nonny told us there wasn't any big secret, but it took us six batches to finally get it right—literally hours of chopping, stirring, stuffing, and "nope." When we finally nailed it, I actually whooped.

And then my brother, because he's a vegetarian, took it a step further. He decided to figure out how to make the gravy without *the giblets*. It's crazy how hard something so simple can be.

I can still hear Nonny saying, "Only a pinch of sage. Any more, it will all turn green."

Some years, we'd go to Nonny's for Thanksgiving because she had the fancy crystal, and, honestly, she really liked being the center of our universe, making so much food and letting us show up with our covered dishes. At her house, she could set her table just the way she liked it, make a fuss over us when we got there.

For my family, Thanksgiving—especially because my mom and dad took in so many families in tough places—meant the blessing of all we shared, the adventures we had, the fact that we knew how to make things work no matter what. Having each other, we understood, was everything.

Mom would always want to do something special or different. One year we used a recipe for Trisha Yearwood's roast turkey that ran in *Country Weekly*, just because I loved Trisha and her singing so much. It's such an easy, can't-screw-it-up way to make a Thanksgiving turkey, and we've cooked some variation of that turkey ever since! Some years my dad'll deep-fry a second turkey too. But deep-fried or not, we still use that recipe pulled out of a long-forgotten country music fan magazine because it's so simple.

In some ways, though, the sides are even better than the turkey. My mom always makes homemade rolls that melt in your mouth. They're so perfect, they don't even need butter. Plus, you need something to sop up the gravy and all the juices from the vegetables, and these are the perfect fluffy, moist, rich rolls.

Vegetables are one of the many beautiful things about how we grew up. Between growing everything ourselves in our garden and how our family cooked them, Luke and I loved *all* vegetables. We couldn't understand kids who didn't like them. And Thanksgiving? For us, that was the greatest parade of vegetable side dishes ever.

When you're excited to see serving bowl after serving bowl of carrots, beans, root vegetables, and potatoes coming to the table as a kid, you grow up to be creative about how you make those things as an adult. Luke sure proves that point. He has an amazing way of making Brussels sprouts, as well as a roasted root vegetable dish with parsnips, carrots, and sweet potatoes that will make you glad you're at the table. There are never leftovers of those!

If we're lucky, somebody makes Princess V's creamed spinach at our Thanksgiving. It's so rich and delicious, it's almost a sin. Still, you can tell yourself you're getting lots of iron and fiber, *and* it's a leafy green vegetable, even if it is slow-cooked in cream and butter.

Over the years, I've started making a broccoli-and-rice casserole; it's become just part of the menu at this point. Plus, I make a sweet potato casserole, which may technically be a vegetable but is almost as good as dessert. We're a family that loves our potatoes. Sweet potatoes, mashed potatoes, scalloped potatoes, yams! You gotta have 'em all.

It's an amazing thing to see the Lambert family spread when it gets laid out. There is food almost everywhere! Back when my parents were building a business, a lot of our daily meals were things you could make pretty fast, so Thanksgiving was a day to really slow down, prep the food, and let it cook slowly. That time spent slow-cooking brought the flavors out, so every flavor could be its best. As a family, we still really enjoy the time invested in the things that take time to prepare, whether we're letting them simmer, bake, or reduce.

We're also a family where converging in the kitchen is how we roll. That is our native habitat. We like to help and enjoy what goes into making food, whether it's chopping, stirring, mixing, or whatever needs doing. And the idea that we're all in it together reinforces being together. Sharing the job of making a meal and then eating it brings us even closer together.

Plus, we're all good eaters. We're healthier eaters now, *maybe*, than we were back when I was growing up. Back then we'd fill up our plates, tell stories, and laugh. Sometimes we'd go right from our big dinner into the pumpkin cookies, pumpkin pie, or pecan pie—sometimes all three! There'd even be pumpkin creamer for the coffee to drink with dessert because, well, it was Thanksgiving, and that Thanksgiving coffee should be special.

Then, like all good Texans, we'd watch the Cowboys play. The Cowboys are very much Texas's team, but on Thanksgiving, that broadcast from Texas Stadium, which is now AT&T Stadium, is every American's Thanksgiving tradition. It doesn't seem to matter who you are, where you're living, or who you normally root for—*everyone* tunes in to watch.

Being that it's us, Dad would get down his guitar. Once dinner was finished, people might stop by to watch the game with us, share some of their special dishes—and get some of ours—and just chat about the day. But

I think a lot of people came over because they knew my dad was gonna play music and sing songs, and that we'd all end up singing along with him. To have good friends, stuffed with turkey and too much pie, singing along to "Angel from Montgomery," is a pretty nice way to finish Thanksgiving.

It's special, the way certain songs have weaved through everything in our world. I think it's a big piece of who we are, but it's also something people from Texas love in a very special, very specific way. There's genuine pride in the artists who come from or speak to how Texans live; it's real storytelling, and honest, with characters you feel like you could know. It's not about being on the radio or having a pop hook, but coming from the heart and showing us the deeper emotions playing out in actual lives. So, anyone who wants to hear Guy Clark or Merle Haggard or whomever they love should come over to our house, because there's a good chance my dad will be playing that guitar and entertaining everyone with the songs they're hoping to hear.

TURKEY

SERVES 10 TO 12

4 tablespoons (½ stick) unsalted butter, softened

One 12-pound turkey, completely thawed and giblets removed

2 tablespoons kosher salt

2 teaspoons freshly ground black pepper

2 celery stalks, cut into lengths to fit inside the turkey cavity

1 medium sweet onion, such as Vidalia, halved

1 large carrot, cut into lengths to fit inside the turkey cavity

2 cups boiling water

ADJUST the oven racks so a covered large roasting pan will fit easily inside. Preheat the oven to 500°F.

RUB the butter on the outside and in the cavity of the turkey. Sprinkle the salt and pepper over the inside and outside of the turkey. Put the celery, onion, and carrot in the cavity. Place the turkey, breast side up, in a large roasting pan. Pour the boiling water into the pan. Cover with a tight-fitting lid and put the pan in the oven.

START a timer for 1 hour when the oven temperature returns to 500°F. Bake for exactly 1 hour, then turn off the oven. *Do not open the oven door!* Leave the turkey in the oven until the oven completely cools; this may take 4 to 6 hours.

RESERVE the pan juices and refrigerate the turkey if it will not be served soon after roasting.

Nonny's THANKSGIVING DRESSING

SERVES 12 TO 14

CORNBREAD

¼ cup vegetable oil

2 cups self-rising cornmeal mix

1¾ cups whole milk

1 large egg, beaten

DRESSING

Cooking spray

4 cups chicken broth

2 large white onions, chopped

2 celery stalks, chopped

1 tablespoon dried sage

1 teaspoon kosher salt

1¼ tablespoons freshly ground black pepper

4 large eggs, beaten

FIRST, make the cornbread. It will need to chill 2 days in the refrigerator.

PREHEAT the oven to 450°F.

HEAT the oil in the oven in an 8-inch cast-iron skillet until shimmering. Meanwhile, in a bowl, stir together the cornmeal, milk, and egg. Carefully pour the hot oil into the bowl and mix. Pour the batter into the skillet, then transfer to the oven and bake for 25 minutes. The cornbread will be light golden brown. Let cool for 5 minutes in the skillet, then transfer to a cooling rack and let sit until completely cool, before crumbling for the dressing.

WHEN the cornbread is ready, make the dressing: Preheat the oven to 450°F. Grease a large roasting pan with cooking spray.

IN a saucepan over high heat, combine the chicken broth with the onions and celery. Bring to a boil, then turn off the heat. When cool, strain the onions and celery, reserving the broth.

ADD the crumbled cornbread to a large bowl, along with the sage, salt, and pepper. Add the eggs and the onion mixture, then add the reserved broth and stir. Pour into the prepared pan and bake, uncovered, until the edges are crusty, 45 minutes to 1 hour. Best served hot, straight out of the oven.

Giblet GRAVY

MAKES 1½ CUPS

Giblets and neck from a whole turkey or chicken

3 cups chicken stock

4 tablespoons (½ stick) unsalted butter

¼ cup all-purpose flour

½ teaspoon kosher salt

½ teaspoon freshly ground black pepper

½ teaspoon poultry seasoning

½ cup half-and-half

2 hard-boiled large eggs, chopped

PLACE the giblets and neck in a saucepan, add the chicken stock, and bring to a boil over high heat. Reduce the heat to low and simmer for 45 minutes to 1 hour. Remove the meat from the stock and let cool. Reserve the stock. When cool enough to handle, finely chop the giblets; remove the meat from the neck and finely chop that too.

MELT the butter in a heavy saucepan over medium heat, then add the flour, salt, pepper, and poultry seasoning. Cook, stirring, for about 3 minutes, until the roux just barely begins to turn golden brown.

SLOWLY stir in 1½ cups of the reserved chicken stock. Stir constantly until it begins to thicken, 5 to 7 minutes, then add the half-and-half. Continue cooking and stirring until thickened. Add the chopped giblets and neck meat and reduce the heat to low. Simmer for 5 minutes. Add the chopped eggs and adjust the seasonings if necessary. Serve warm.

Scalloped POTATOES

SERVES 4 TO 6

1 teaspoon kosher salt, plus more for boiling

3 pounds new potatoes, cut into 1-inch cubes

4 tablespoons (½ stick) unsalted butter, cut into cubes

8 ounces Velveeta, cubed

1 cup shredded cheddar cheese

½ teaspoon freshly ground black pepper

½ cup sour cream

¼ cup whole milk

Parsley or 3 green onions, sliced

PREHEAT the oven to 350°F.

PLACE the potatoes in a pot of cold salted water. Bring to a boil and cook until almost soft, 10 to 12 minutes.

PLACE the butter evenly across the bottom of a 9 x 13-inch casserole dish. Layer with half of the potatoes, half of the Velveeta, and half of the cheddar. Season with ½ teaspoon of the salt and ¼ teaspoon of the pepper. Dot with the sour cream, then repeat layering with the remaining potatoes, the remaining ½ teaspoon salt and ¼ teaspoon pepper, Velveeta, and cheddar. Pour the milk over the entire casserole. Top with the parsley or green onions. Bake, uncovered, until bubbly, about 30 minutes. Serve right out of the oven.

Sweet Potato
CASSEROLE

SERVES 6 TO 8

½ cup (1 stick) unsalted butter, melted, plus 1 tablespoon for greasing

3 cups mashed sweet potatoes, cooled

FOR THE PECAN TOPPING

½ cup light brown sugar

⅓ cup all-purpose flour

½ cup whole milk

1 cup light brown sugar

1 teaspoon vanilla extract

2 large eggs, lightly beaten

4 tablespoons (½ stick) unsalted butter, melted

1 cup chopped pecans

PREHEAT the oven to 350°F. Grease a 9 x 12-inch casserole dish with the 1 tablespoon of butter.

IN a large bowl, stir together the melted butter, potatoes, milk, brown sugar, vanilla, and eggs until well combined. Pour into the prepared casserole.

MAKE the pecan topping: In a separate bowl, stir together the brown sugar, flour, butter, and pecans until well combined. Pour the topping over the filling in the casserole. Bake for 35 to 40 minutes, until set in the center and golden on top. Delicious right out of the oven.

Pumpkin Spice
COFFEE CREAMER

MAKES 1 QUART

2 cups half-and-half or unsweetened almond milk

1 (14-ounce) can sweetened condensed milk (I like Eagle brand)

¼ cup canned pure pumpkin puree

2 teaspoons ground cinnamon

2 teaspoons pumpkin pie spice

2 teaspoons vanilla extract

¼ teaspoon ground ginger

IN a bowl, whisk together the half-and-half or almond milk, the condensed milk, pumpkin, cinnamon, pumpkin pie spice, vanilla, and ginger. Pour into a 1-quart canning jar, seal, and store in the refrigerator for 2 to 3 weeks. Shake well before serving.

CHRISTMAS

Christmas is—and always was—big doings at our house. Not so much because of the presents, because we never had that kind of money. For us, Christmas was all about the idea of love, the joy of the season, and celebrating family. Plus, the chance to do all that Christmas decorating? *That* was a big deal to Mom, who got her hard-core black diamond ski run rush from making our house Christmas central.

Just going out to chop down a Christmas tree was epic. We lived out in the country, so Daddy'd take me out in the woods to pick "just the right one," because we both knew you'd need *just* the right one for when Santa came! Christmas was all around us, everywhere—you just had to see it. It was such a great gift to give a little girl.

This was especially true in those years when things weren't so good for our family. Christmas was really important. In tough times, people say, "Well, at least we've got each other." It sounds like a cliché, but I can promise you it's true.

Lots of people talk about the fancy things, the big trips or whatever expensive presents they're looking for at the holidays. I don't understand that. Never have. That's not to say Christmas gifts don't matter. I think about the year of "*The Lion King* Christmas" and just smile. We *all* still talk about that.

Understand, we were pretty poor back then, but I didn't know it. My mom made sure we had no idea. We'd finally gotten into the House That Built Me, which started out more as the Wreck We Lived In. She had a vision for how to make that house a home, to use that land to nourish and teach us. We had everything we needed, and we believed it was the greatest place we could ever be.

In that spirit of plenty, Mom was determined we were going to have the most amazing Christmas that first year in our new house. Without missing a beat, Beverly went on down to the Dollar General store, and I swear she bought every last thing she could find that was made from, looked like, or actually was tied to *The Lion King*.

We'd worn out the poor guy at the Blockbuster Video store, going in and renting that movie over and over. It was the only thing Luke and I wanted to watch. There is so much hope to the story, plus Luke and I loved the music. So when things seemed to be going sideways instead of down, Mom decided we were going to have a big, beautiful Christmas. We knew we were in a good place, that's true. But we were still kids. Yes, we loved our new home and felt how much the family cared about us. Still, you get your hopes up. You can't help it.

I have to tell you: when Luke and I raced down to the tree Christmas morning and saw all that haul, we were sure we'd cleaned up and won the lottery! My mom had *Lion King everything*, absolutely *everywhere*. It was the most unbelievable sight: piles and stacks of stuffed animals, pajamas, beach towels, throw blankets, tissues, lip balm, candy, and gum—*all* of it with Simba and our other favorite characters from the movie we couldn't get enough of. Even if the stuff was cheap, maybe out of date, we didn't care. Suddenly, we had lots and lots of something we really loved!

It's hard to believe how many things were created to market that movie. We didn't see it that way, though. We just saw our very favorite story, in all these different ways, all wrapped with pretty bows. Those gifts were everything we could've ever wanted.

That's the thing about the holidays, you know? Some people give practical things. Some people give ridiculously expensive things. What we learned growing up is to believe that the best thing for the holidays is being together, laughing and loving on each other.

On Christmas Eve, we'd be over at Nonny's doing traditional Christmas dinner. It was just like Thanksgiving, but with a ham. We'd be told exactly what to bring, and that's exactly what we brought. That dinner would be formal and fancy, but the rest? Well, we'd do Christmas Eve night and Christmas Day *our* way.

When we got a little older and my parents' business started coming together, we'd have prime rib with the most delicious horseradish sauce and all the fixings: roasted potatoes, Brussels sprouts, Vicki's creamed spinach. It was very grown-up and very elegant, but still very us.

It's funny what you remember, and also there are those moments you never forget. There's a difference. Some memories you choose to remember, while some things just subconsciously embed in your mind. So much of who we all were when things weren't so good actually made my brother (who's now a chef) and me who we are today. It's why we now look at everything as an adventure, every day as a gift. For me, I got the stories and values to make my music out of. Again, that's everything Nicolle Galyon and Natalie Hemby and I were trying to put into "Automatic," which won the Academy of Country Music Song of the Year and Country Music Association Single of the Year, because a lot of people felt it too. We were writing not just about how things used to be, but why those things were so much sweeter, when we landed on the line, "If you had something to say, you'd write it on a piece of paper / Then you put a stamp on it / And they'd get it three days later."

After we'd go cut down a tree, Mom would make Christmas ornaments out of dried fruit and cinnamon sticks. She'd make paper chains, sometimes with colored paper, sometimes with paper she'd spray-paint gold. We'd add popcorn strings and tinsel. It was way more do-it-yourself, but the do-it-ourselves was part of the fun.

There were so many little Christmas things we just loved. Anyone could do them, but they were our little things. We used to make no-flour Magic Peanut Butter Cookies for Santa. They have only four ingredients but are the crunchiest, easiest, yummiest things. A cup of crunchy—*must be crunchy*—peanut butter, a cup of sugar, one egg, and a teaspoon of vanilla. That was it! Ten minutes on 350°F and—BOOM!—cookies for

Santa. When you're little, something that simple makes you very excited about getting ready for Mr. Claus.

When we got older and found out *who* Santa was, we swapped cinnamon eggnog for the milk. Even more importantly, because these cookies are so wickedly delicious, we realized we needed to cut down on the number of cookies. My dad could eat twelve of them, no problem. He wouldn't have wanted us thinking Santa didn't like what we left him, which would've been a whole other problem. But my mom had other tricks. She used to tell us that because Santa was going to so many houses, we should only put out maybe four cookies. That way my dad wouldn't gain too much weight playing Santa.

On Christmas morning, we would run full-on down the stairs to see what had happened while we were sleeping. Mom would be doing her part, too, creating special breakfast treats. She'd have hot chocolate with marshmallows, or sometimes doughnuts cut out of canned biscuit dough. She'd crack that biscuit can's seal, break 'em apart, then take a small jar and pull out the middle of each one. Next thing you knew, she'd be frying 'em up in one of Daddy's cast-iron skillets, draining 'em on paper towels, and rolling 'em in sugar. Some years she'd make us Mickey Mouse pancakes, only we couldn't afford—or maybe they just didn't make—a mold, so she'd stand there and free-pour those Mickeys right onto the griddle with this great big smile on her face. One larger pour, two littler ones, then a spatula to the batter before it cooked into something solid.

It makes me smile thinking about what you can do if you just get a little creative. My mom was the queen of this. I don't think any of us ever had one thought about what we didn't have. We were always laughing and wondering how we could *do* whatever it was we wanted to do. How do you make it? How do you get there? What's that flavor? There was never a doubt. Those are things you can't put a price tag on, and I swear they only got more priceless every year. Every memory makes you richer, so take these and use them too.

Creamy
BACON BRUSSELS SPROUTS

SERVES 4 TO 6

1 pound Brussels sprouts, trimmed and halved lengthwise

2 tablespoons extra-virgin olive oil

1 teaspoon sea salt, plus more as needed

½ teaspoon freshly ground black pepper, plus more as needed

4 slices bacon, chopped

1 shallot, chopped

1 cup cremini mushrooms, chopped

1 clove garlic, minced

¼ cup cream sherry

½ cup heavy cream

PREHEAT the oven to 475°F.

ON a parchment-lined baking sheet, toss the Brussels sprouts with the olive oil, salt, and pepper. Roast until browned, about 15 minutes.

MEANWHILE, heat a large, deep skillet over medium-high heat. Add the bacon and cook, stirring occasionally, until beginning to brown at the edges, 5 to 8 minutes. Reduce the heat to medium and stir in the shallot and mushrooms. Cook until the shallots are translucent, about 5 minutes. Sprinkle in the garlic and cook for 1 minute. Stir in the sherry and cream, bring the mixture to a boil, and cook, stirring, until the liquid is reduced by half, about 2 minutes. The sauce should coat the back of a spoon.

TRANSFER the roasted Brussels sprouts to the skillet and toss to coat. Season with salt and pepper to taste before serving.

Roasted
ROOT VEGETABLE
WINTER SALAD

SERVES 6 TO 8

2 sweet potatoes, peeled and cubed

1 acorn squash, seeded and cubed

2 tablespoons extra-virgin olive oil

1 tablespoon kosher salt

DRESSING

1 tablespoon extra-virgin olive oil

1 tablespoon sriracha

2 tablespoons maple syrup

1 tablespoon honey

1 tablespoon balsamic vinegar

1 clove garlic, minced

GARNISHES

1 avocado, halved, pitted, and cubed

Pomegranate seeds

Toasted pumpkin seeds

Crumbled queso fresco

Fresh cilantro leaves

PREHEAT the oven to 400°F.

PLACE the sweet potatoes and acorn squash on a parchment-lined baking sheet. Toss with the olive oil and salt. Roast for 30 to 35 minutes, until the potatoes and squash are tender and golden.

MEANWHILE, make the dressing: In a small bowl, whisk together the olive oil, sriracha, maple syrup, honey, vinegar, and garlic.

WHEN the squash and sweet potatoes are done cooking, let cool for a few minutes, then arrange on a platter and drizzle with the dressing. Top with the avocado, pomegranate seeds, pumpkin seeds, and crumbled queso fresco. Garnish with cilantro leaves before serving.

Magic
PEANUT BUTTER COOKIES
FOR SANTA

MAKES 15 COOKIES

1 cup crunchy peanut butter

1 cup sugar

1 large egg

1 teaspoon vanilla extract

PREHEAT the oven to 350°F. Line a baking sheet with parchment paper.

IN a large bowl, mix together the peanut butter, sugar, egg, and vanilla until well combined. Roll the dough into 15 balls (see Tip) and transfer to the prepared baking sheet, spaced about 2 inches apart. Using a fork, make a crisscross pattern in each ball of dough—this will also flatten them into a cookie shape. Bake for 10 to 15 minutes. Bake until the cookies are browned along the edges, but not on top. Remove from the oven and let cool on the baking sheet.

TIP: *Oil your hands before rolling the dough into balls.*

EASTER

Easter was an extravaganza! Beyond the Easter eggs and the candy, there was the controlled chaos of the official church Easter egg hunt, followed by the always-too-much-everything, delicious church potluck. *Then* we'd go to Nonny's for her sit-down Easter dinner. Then, if we hadn't had Easter brunch before church, we'd have something easy when we got home for the friends who came by.

Nonny was hilarious on Easter. She would come to church decked out, looking just perfect. She'd always leave right after services ended. She'd rush off, saying she had to get home to make her "special cheesecake." She would be whipping up a batch of her world-famous cherry salad. Once you tasted it, you'd want it at *every* get-together. It was cherry pie filling, whipped cream, and crushed pineapple all mixed together with sweetened condensed milk, then put in the fridge. And so, off she would go, year after year. Truth is, Nonny wanted to stay home and have a little bourbon before we got there. That felt a lot better to her than watching squealing kids chase after colored eggs and a whole bunch of casseroles. She loved a lot of stuff, but that was not her thing.

Easter potluck at church was a bit like full-contact wrestling. All the church ladies would bring their very best casseroles and desserts. There would be tables, all covered in Pyrex dishes, Fiestaware casseroles, and all sorts of platters in every shape and size. To Luke and me, it was the greatest buffet ever. You'd have vegetable casseroles, special chicken casseroles, Mexican dishes, Jell-O salads with fruit, Jell-O salads with fruit *and* whipped cream, salad salads, and really delicious tuna fish or ham salad with Ritz crackers.

Those church ladies would come in their best outfits, bringing their best dishes, determined to have the yummiest item on the whole table. It was outrageous, seeing that Easter spread, and we'd try to cram as much as possible onto our plates.

It was loud, with all the little kids racing around looking for the eggs that had been hidden. Maybe we were a little jacked up on those foil-covered chocolate eggs. I can't remember. (Wink.)

My mom made sure we had "outfits," real Easter outfits. Some years, she made my dress, because she knew *exactly* what she wanted. When it came to church, Mom was serious. She'd have her giant hair and fanciest dress, and so did I. The four of us would roll into the church hall for that buffet, looking like we'd thought through our whole look.

There are a couple things about Easter we should get out of the way early.

1. My mom believes the easiest way to get children to eat vegetables are her Bunny Eggs.
2. Easter eggs are big fun to dye, and there's no reason everyone can't do it.
3. There's nothing better for Easter than a Bunny Cake! Absolutely, yes, we're gonna get into some Bunny Cake.

BEFORE CITY PEOPLE THOUGHT IT WAS COOL TO KEEP CHICKENS, WE had chickens. They were mostly for eggs, but occasionally a young rooster would become dinner. Eggs are a good source of protein, and the chickens were pretty funny to watch too. When I was a kid, I'd go out and feed them, gather up the eggs. We had all kinds of kinds: Ameraucanas; Dominicans and Leghorns with their red, red combs; these ridiculously beautiful jet-black Ortholopes; Rhode Island Reds. There was just always a big variety! They'd be running around the yard, leaving us their beautiful, dark fresh eggs. To this day, I've never tasted anything close to one of our hen's fresh eggs.

As you know by this point, deviled eggs for us are practically *another* food group. Having a special deviled egg dish to serve them on is a true mark of a Southern woman. For Easter, deviled eggs go to a whole new level. Mom goes all out. She makes little animals out of the eggs and decorates them, and, naturally, she especially likes making bunnies.

When I was a kid, it wouldn't have been Easter without my mom's Bunny Eggs—so much so, I now find myself making them for friends, or friends with kids, or friends who really are just big kids. I remember seeing those faces light up when my mom'd come in with a plateful of "bunnies," using a little piece of carrot for the nose, little bits of green or red pepper for the mouth and eyes; if you wanted hair or eyebrows, you'd use a little bit of broccoli. Then the ears would be celery or more peppers.

She could do three dozen, four, five in a couple hours! She'd say, "It's no more time than a cake, and it's a lot better for those kids to eat."

She'd recycle our Easter eggs for her deviled eggs. We'd find 'em, then she'd crack 'em open, cut 'em in half, scrape out those incredibly yellow yolks, and start making the filling. Watching, or chopping and being part of the egg/animal transformation, was as much fun as dyeing the eggs in the first place—and dyeing Easter eggs is pretty fun. We laid everything out in the kitchen with newspapers on the tables and a bunch of red Solo cups filled with food coloring, hot water, and a little vinegar.

We'd decorate the eggs with stickers, glitter, or crayons, so the dye didn't stick in those spots, then plop them into the cups and wait. Obviously, the longer we'd leave them, the darker the color would be. Or you might take one out, let it dry, then put it in another cup.

We could be as creative as we dreamed. There are so many ways to engage a kid's imagination. My mom and dad were both so good at that.

Bunny Cake is all imagination. It can be super simple with a few obvious tricks, or it can be homemade everything with special elements that take the bunny over the top. When I was a little girl, I was just excited when Mom gave us a box of mix and a can of icing. We'd get two round cake pans, cook the cakes by the directions, then turn one of the cakes out from the pan and let that be the face; then we'd cut out the ears, the bow tie, and the bunny paws from another circle pan of yellow cake.

That's how simple our Bunny Cake is: a one-layer cake with a little creativity. If you're making the icing from scratch, it's about the powdered sugar, the butter, and a little vanilla. But that's *not* the deal. The *deal* is how you decorate your rabbit. First, you *must* have coconut for his fur. Some people like flakes, others prefer shredded. Either way, coconut is how you make your bunny real. Then you're going to need a couple Hershey's Kisses for his eyes. They stick up from the icing and the coconut and make the bunny seem so very interested in what's going on.

You need black licorice whips for his whiskers and red whips or licorice sticks to make his little mouth. You can use red gumdrops for his mouth instead, but the black licorice whips for his whiskers are the most fun. Oh, and you need one little piece of candy corn for his nose.

All bunnies need buttons. We used Dots gumdrops growing up. They came in red, yellow, green, and orange. Not everybody likes them because they're so chewy, so you can substitute M&M's if you like those better. Or, if you want something minty fresh, try Junior Mints. Or maybe those red raspberry gumdrops. Gummy bears could work for a rave rabbit, maybe.

If you take a little time, you can create a really cute little Easter bunny—and impress your friends.

I know. I made a Bunny Cake last year for my band and crew. They thought it was the sweetest thing they'd ever seen. It was such a little thing to do, but seeing everyone's smiles? *That* made *me* feel good. Sometimes, something as simple and darling as this cake can show how much you care.

Neicy's BUNNY BREAD

SERVES 10 TO 12

Cooking spray

2 (1-pound) loaves frozen bread
dough, thawed

2 raisins

2 almond slices

1 large egg, beaten with
1 tablespoon water

Lettuce leaves, dip, and sliced
fresh vegetables, for serving

GREASE a large rimmed baking sheet with cooking spray.

SLICE a quarter off the first loaf of bread dough and form into a pear shape
for the bunny's head. Shape the remainder of the loaf into an oval for the
bunny's body. Place both pieces on the prepared baking sheet. With a knife,
make narrow cuts on each side of the head for whiskers.

CUT the second loaf of bread dough into four equal pieces. Shape two
pieces into 16-inch ropes for the bunny's ears. Fold each rope in half and
arrange on top of the head. Cut a third piece of dough in half, then shape
each half into ovals for the back paws. Cut two slits on top of each for toes.
Position on each side of the body. Cut the last piece of dough into three
equal pieces. Shape two of them into ovals for the front paws. Cut two slits
on top of each for toes. Shape the remaining piece of dough into three small
balls, two for the cheeks and one for the nose. (This should be a slightly
smaller ball than the other two.) Position them on the face. Add the raisins
for eyes and almonds for teeth.

BRUSH the dough with the beaten egg. Cover and let rise until doubled, approximately 60 to 90 minutes.

PREHEAT the oven to 350°F.

BAKE the bread for 25 to 30 minutes. Let cool on the baking sheet, then transfer to a large platter. Scoop out the belly (center) of the bunny's body. To serve, line the empty belly with lettuce leaves and fill with your favorite dip. Surround the bunny with fresh vegetables.

Honey-Glazed
CARROTS

SERVES 6 TO 8

Cooking spray

5 tablespoons unsalted butter

4 cloves garlic, minced

2 tablespoons honey

2 pounds carrots, peeled and cut on the diagonal into 2- to 3-inch pieces

½ teaspoon kosher salt, plus more as needed

¼ teaspoon freshly ground black pepper, plus more as needed

Chopped fresh parsley, for garnish

PREHEAT the oven to 425°F. Grease a rimmed baking sheet with cooking spray.

IN a large nonstick skillet over medium heat, melt the butter. Add the garlic and cook for 3 minutes, stirring frequently, until lightly browned. (Be careful *not* to burn the garlic!) Remove from the heat and stir in the honey until thoroughly combined.

YOU can either toss the carrots in the sauce right in the skillet or pour the sauce over the carrots in a large bowl. Season with the salt and pepper and stir until well combined.

TRANSFER the carrots to the prepared baking sheet, arranging them in a single layer. Bake for 25 to 30 minutes, until the carrots are browned and tender.

TRANSFER to a serving plate, taste for seasonings, and adjust accordingly. Garnish with parsley before serving.

Caterpillar and Bunny
CAKES

SERVES 8 TO 10

Cooking spray

All-purpose flour, for dusting

1 (15-ounce) box yellow cake mix
(I like Betty Crocker Super Moist)

1 (8-ounce) can crushed pineapple
with juices

½ cup water

⅓ cup vegetable oil

3 large eggs

2 teaspoons rum extract

1 (12-ounce) container whipped
white frosting (I like Betty
Crocker)

¼ cup unsweetened flaked coconut

Food coloring for the frosting,
extra coconut, tube frosting, and
candies of your choice, such as
Dots, M&M's, licorice, chocolate
chips, for decorating

PREHEAT the oven to 350°F (325°F for dark or nonstick pans). Grease with
cooking spray and lightly flour the bottoms and sides of two 8- or 9-inch
round cake pans for bunny cake or one Bundt cake pan for caterpillar.

IN a large bowl, using an electric mixer on low speed, beat the cake mix,
pineapple, water, oil, eggs, and 1 teaspoon of the rum extract for 2 minutes,
scraping down the side of the bowl occasionally. Be careful not to overbeat.
Divide the batter among the prepared pans. Bake according to the cake
mix directions. Let the cakes cool completely in the pans. The cakes will
need to be cut to form the animals. Use the photos—and of course, your
imagination!—as a guide.

STIR the remaining 1 teaspoon rum extract into the frosting. With an offset
spatula, spread the frosting over the tops and sides of the cakes. Sprinkle
evenly with the flaked coconut.

HALLOWEEN

Halloween was a mixed bag when I was little.

But that taught me a lot about not being stuck on one idea of what a holiday should be. Because of Nonny and her friends, I'd almost have rather gone over to her house than gone trick-or-treating. Crazy, right? What little kid wants to hang out with older people instead of running around demanding candy? Me. Maybe it was my old soul.

My mom, who could do anything and often had to, figured out how to make my brother and me super-cute costumes every year. We didn't have the money to go out and buy the costumes in boxes with plastic masks like most of the kids wore; instead, our mom turned us into magical things. I think my favorite was either the scarecrow or the hobo. These were easy, and she could whip them up without too much stress. Put us in some loose jeans, an undershirt, then a flannel shirt, and stuff everything with straw. Then she'd put a floppy straw hat on our heads, use an eye pencil or mascara to give us a black triangle nose, and use an eyebrow pencil for some freckles. One of us would get a corncob pipe and the other was handed a broomstick. Voilà! Scarecrows.

If we were going to be hoboes, she'd put us in some of my dad's old clothes, take a pair of suspenders, roll up the sleeves on a shirt that was entirely too big, and maybe add an old jacket. She had this perfect sense of how to make us look like ramblers ridin' the rails. Then she'd draw a little beard on our chins or make our faces a little dirty, and add an old felt fedora or bowler hat she'd picked up along the way. Suddenly, we were straight out of Roger Miller's "King of the Road."

We were picture-perfect scarecrows or hoboes, far more realistic than the kids in the highly flammable Spider-Man onesies, with the plastic masks you could barely see through.

But the real fun was over at Nonny's. Those witches *knew* how to do it. Now, Wanda and her pals Pat and Kay got dressed up like nasty old witches every year, all black and lumpy. And, boy, did they get into the makeup hard. They thought it was hilarious to hide and jump out at the kids in the neighborhood. They'd scare them two-thirds to death; when kids would start screaming, Nonny, Kay, and Pat would be cackling like witches. They thought it was the funniest thing ever. Of course, once they scared 'em, they'd give those little kids all kinds of candy. Not just one crummy piece, but a handful! It was kind of a "no hard feelings" offering, but also a reminder: on Halloween, all's fair in trick-*or*-treating.

Nonny and her crew would start their transformation late in the afternoon, getting into their wardrobe and makeup. They might also have a light Canadian Hunter grown-up drink, as well as a few cigarettes, while they got ready. And if I was over there, they'd dress me up like a junior witch or a witch's apprentice. I'd be a mini-them, only with fewer warts.

To be part of their posse when they were getting ready was like being in a secret society. I never joined a sorority, but this felt like the same kind of thing. The special rituals, the being together and knowing the secrets— and, yes, hazing the freshman. Not a lot, just enough to give me a little fright, then a bunch of candy.

It's all part of what Halloween is: the squeals and the sweets, the tricks to earn your treats. But the truth is, nobody would've dared trick Nonny.

Even today, there's something I love about Halloween and getting to pretend to be someone else for a few hours, running a little amok with your friends. We don't need much of an excuse, to be honest, but what's not to love about getting all dressed up and having some fun?!

Pumpkin
OATMEAL CHOCOLATE CHIP COOKIES

MAKES 5 OR 6 DOZEN

¾ pound (3 sticks) unsalted butter, softened

2 cups packed light brown sugar

1 cup granulated sugar

1 (15-ounce) can pure pumpkin puree

1 large egg

1 teaspoon vanilla extract

4 cups all-purpose flour

2 cups quick-cooking oats

2 teaspoons ground cinnamon

2 teaspoons pumpkin pie spice

2 teaspoons baking soda

1 teaspoon baking powder

1 teaspoon salt

2 cups miniature chocolate chips

1 cup finely chopped walnuts or pecans (optional)

PREHEAT the oven to 375°F. Line 2 baking sheets with parchment paper.

IN the bowl of an electric mixer (or using a hand mixer), beat together the butter and both sugars until creamy. Beat in the pumpkin, egg, and vanilla, scraping down the sides of the bowl as necessary, until smooth.

IN a large bowl, mix together the flour, oats, cinnamon, pumpkin pie spice, baking soda, baking powder, and salt. Stir the dry ingredients into the wet ingredients until well combined. Fold in the chocolate chips and nuts, if using.

USE a 2-tablespoon-size cookie scoop to drop balls of dough, spaced a couple inches apart, onto the prepared baking sheets. Bake for 10 to 12 minutes. The cookies will be soft-centered with crispy edges. Transfer to a wire rack to cool completely. Repeat with the remaining dough until all the cookies are baked.

Buckshot CHILI

SERVES 8 TO 10

2 pounds ground beef, preferably chili grind, or ground venison

1 pound ground chuck

2 tablespoons extra-virgin olive oil

1 yellow onion, chopped

1 white onion, chopped

1 jalapeño, diced (optional)

1 (28-ounce) can diced tomatoes

1 (10-ounce) can diced tomatoes with green chiles (I like Ro-Tel)

1½ teaspoons hot pepper sauce, such as Tabasco

¼ cup chili powder

2 teaspoons ground cumin

2 teaspoons garlic powder

1 teaspoon kosher salt

2½ teaspoons freshly ground black pepper

1 (15-ounce) can pinto beans, undrained (optional)

Topping suggestions: cheese, onions, sour cream, cilantro, and Fritos

1 recipe Jalapeño Cornbread (opposite), for serving

IN a large skillet, working in batches if necessary, cook the ground meat, breaking it up with a wooden spoon, until browned, 5 to 7 minutes. Set aside.

IN a large stockpot, heat the oil over medium-high heat. Add the onions and jalapeño, if using, and sauté for 3 to 5 minutes. Add the browned meat, the tomatoes, hot sauce, chili powder, cumin, garlic powder, salt, and pepper. Bring to a boil, then reduce the heat to low and simmer for 3 hours. Add the beans, if using, and simmer on low for an additional hour.

LADLE the chili into bowls, garnish with the desired toppings, and serve with Jalapeño Cornbread.

Jalapeño CORNBREAD

SERVES 6 TO 8

Cooking spray

2 cups cornbread mix

2 tablespoons sugar

1 teaspoon kosher salt

¼ cup whole milk

4 large eggs

⅔ cup vegetable oil

1 small yellow onion, chopped

1 (14.75-ounce) can cream-style corn

⅔ cup grated medium cheddar cheese

¼ cup canned pickled jalapeños, chopped

PREHEAT the oven to 450°F. Grease a 9 x 13-inch baking dish with cooking spray.

IN a large bowl, combine the cornbread mix, sugar, and salt. In a separate bowl, combine the milk, eggs, and oil. Stir the wet ingredients into the dry ingredients until mostly smooth. Mix in the onion, corn, cheese, and jalapeños.

POUR the batter into the prepared baking dish. Bake for 25 to 30 minutes, until a toothpick inserted in the center comes out clean.

10

JUST DESSERTS

▼▼▼▼▼▼▼▼▼▼▼▼▼▼▼▼▼▼▼▼▼▼▼

When Only Something Chocolate, Peanut Butter, and Delicious Will Do

I love dessert. Chocolate cake, Nonny's cookies, and especially a really good banana split. Growing up, we didn't have dessert unless it was a special occasion—Christmas, Thanksgiving, a birthday, or a celebration. So, for us, dessert was always a real treat.

Even now, when we do it, we *do* it. To give you an idea how serious dessert is to all of us, let's talk about glamping. When we load up the Airstreams, or even just head to the river or go tailgating, Vicki actually has specific cupcake towers. They are made of plastic or melamine, so they're safe for traveling and for outdoor use. Princess V is known for both her amazing cupcake stands and her cupcakes. When she comes to parties, she's got them in colors, themes, and even different sizes. It's no different when she's out in the wild. She's never going to just pull her cupcakes out of a Tupperware and put 'em on a paper plate. Never! She's going to give her world-famous cupcakes the presentation they deserve.

I'm a classic American girl when it comes to desserts. I am not really a tiramisu person, which some people think is a crime. But give me a sheet cake or some ice cream, I'm thrilled. Even better would be to put some Dutch Oven Campfire Cobbler on the campfire, and you'll see me get the biggest grin on my face.

It's the classics, or the basics. They're delicious, and every bite takes you back to a place and a time. Just like those flourless peanut butter cookies we'd leave out for Santa. They were so good because of all the ingredients and caring that went into them.

The recipe came from Mom's aunt Margie, who lived out in Balch Springs, Texas. She really got my mom into country and western music back when. In 1978, she and Mom made this recipe that was almost too easy.

Making those cookies is actually my very first memory of cooking with my mom. It was so simple, there couldn't have been a better place to start cooking! I was such a little girl, I had to stand on a chair to be tall enough to reach the counter. But even a small child can measure a cup of crunchy peanut butter, a cup of sugar, one teaspoon of vanilla, and an egg—and when you do, you're making delicious cookies!

See what I mean for a perfect way to start? You mix it all up, turn the oven to 350 degrees. When it's preheated, you scoop little spoonfuls of yumminess onto a greased cookie sheet. Like magic, at four and five years old I was in the kitchen with my mom doing something where I was the actual person cooking instead of just passing the ingredients to a grown-up.

Another classic: the legendary Nonny Cookies. They're so good, those perfect chocolate chip cookies, that when I was playing "Kerosene" at the 2005 CMA Awards, Mom brought me a whole bag of them for my twenty-second birthday. She carried them all the way to New York City in her purse, so they wouldn't get crushed. They were truly a treasure!

I remember when I was growing up, Mom knew how to make dessert awesome. Even though baking wasn't her thing, she managed to balance it all. I have memories of her on the phone, working on a case, checking records or taking notes, with cookies in the oven because she was our school room mom and cookies were called for.

When she didn't have time, Mom would find solutions even more fun than having some big ol' cake. This is especially important when you've got a houseful of children who know how to eat dessert 'til their tummies hurt. One day she bought *all* the stuff for banana splits. That is a massive presentation when you're dealing with ten or fifteen kids! She got all the sauces, sprinkles, coconut, nuts, and cherries for the top, and lined them all up in little bowls or teacups. Suddenly, it wasn't just dessert, it was quite the production. Add making little mountains of whipped cream from the can all over it, and there are no words for how fancy it all feels.

Whenever I'd have slumber parties or Luke would have people over, banana splits were the first line of defense. They didn't take a lot of work; the kids could pretty much build their own *and* everybody was so happy with what they had. Plus, for less than $30, everybody could gorge themselves and truly be happy—and you might have enough left over to do it again.

When I was in high school, I used to joke that I got by on my really high ponytail. In cheerleading, I couldn't jump very high, so I literally wore a high ponytail to look taller. I already knew my heart and my dreams were in music, so that's where my energy went. I eventually petitioned to join a program called Operation Graduation. I got my diploma early so I could chase my songs. But while I was still in school, I took lots of basics to fulfill my requirements.

One of those classes was home economics. I was a junior and needed more elective credits. It's not a dumb class, exactly, but it's not calculus or quantum physics. In reality, some of what you learn in home economics is pretty valuable, but you don't know that when you're fifteen—and bored. You learn to cook, to balance a checkbook, some basic life skills you'll need to "run a home."

Somehow, I got voted the vice president of home ec, which meant leading one class, which didn't seem like a very big commitment. And on any day the president wasn't there, I'd be the student leader with the teacher.

There was only one small wrinkle: the president got pregnant. Suddenly, I became president. That's a whole other deal. The person who is president of home ec is usually someone who really *loves* home ec, not someone who is just filling out their schedule with easy classes.

Mostly, the people in the class were either Goody Two-Shoes who did everything perfectly or stoners who didn't want to work that hard. That was the good news: expectations were low. But I still had to figure out what we were going to do in each of the student-led classes, because you have to fill out the rest of semester.

Someone came in for one whole class to teach us how to make meatloaf. Now, it wasn't the Loaf or anything like it, but one day someone literally came in and showed a room full of high school kids the basics of taking a pound of ground meat and turning it into something tastier than just a slab of meat on a plate.

For one class, though, I decided I was going for it. I was going to teach everyone how to make our family's Hummingbird Cake, which to this day is one of Mom's signature dishes. When I'm going to party at a friend's house, I like to bring this cake with me. Most people have never tasted anything like it, and it looks so pretty when you put it on the table. It's a real showstopper for sure. With its cream cheese icing, all the pineapple, and the nuts, it's so cinnamony good. Once you've had a slice, you're going to want another.

To give you an idea of how special this cake is: we actually had a thing called Countryfest in Lindale on the second Saturday in October. It's a reason to have a community event for our small town, with a parade featuring every club and team. They always have an honest-to-goodness Cakewalk as one of the big highlights. All the ladies get their best recipes and go to town.

For me, the first time I ever tried to make that Hummingbird Cake was for that Countryfest Cakewalk. I figured if I was going to enter a cake, I wanted to go big or go home—and I knew anyone who tasted it would die, because it's got all those flavors wrapped up in cream cheese icing. It's versatile too. It's the kind of cake you can make a couple different ways—in a Bundt pan or as a double layer cake. When you cook it as a Bundt, it feels a little less formal and more like a coffee cake, or something you can slice and top with ice cream or pineapple sherbet. When you cook it in two cake pans, then stack it up with the layers of icing on top, it's definitely a more formal sort of cake. That's when it looks like a really official, cover-of-a-cookbook kind of dessert.

I'm not sure which way is better, honestly, but when you see either version, you know immediately that someone actually took the time to measure all those ingredients, add the rest of the stuff, mix it up, then pour it in the pans and let it bake, cool, and assemble. It's not a fancy bakery cake, even though it looks gorgeous; it's something someone made just for this moment.

The Hummingbird Cake has a really interesting origin for us. It's one of our stories we tell each other that says plenty about who we are, *and* it's hilarious. The recipe is from my aunt who's not in the family any longer. She'd married into our family, but then got a divorce and moved away. We were all talking about how much we missed that cake, and one thing led to another. Ultimately, Nonny decided we shouldn't be doing without it.

So, like only she could, she called my aunt up—just picked up the phone, got past the pleasantries, and said, "I'm so sorry about everything that happened. It was all such a shame, but I was wondering if we could have your green bean casserole and Hummingbird Cake recipes. They were just so delicious."

Damned if that woman didn't just give her the recipes. She went and got out her exact measurements and read 'em to Nonny right there over the phone, which says something. Perhaps she was proud that we loved her dishes so much, or maybe it was the mere power of Nonny being Nonny, which meant getting people to do whatever it was she thought needed doing! Either way, and I do think people love the idea that something they've cooked for you made such an impression that you'd call an ex-wife/former family member to ask for the recipe.

Yes, chicken and sausage on the grill is the essence of love to me, but there's something about all the special treats Nonny, Mom, Vicki, Heidi, and Denise made that really taste like the sweetness in all these women's hearts. They could be salty, feisty, crazy, tough, funny, butt-busting hard workers, but in the end, their love is always there when you need it most (though sometimes they won't even admit it because Texans are sneaky that way).

There's nothing like the Fischer sisters' rum balls. Vicki, especially, is the one who you can always count on for the boozy desserts! Princess V just knows how to liquor up that last course like nobody else. You haven't lived until you've had a whiskey cupcake! It takes something you think you know, something everybody loves, then gives it a little spin. The look of surprise when that whiskey taste hits folks' tongues? It's not what people expect. It's even better. Their eyes light up, the corners of their mouths turn up; they can't get that second bite fast enough. And for those who say they don't really like desserts or sweets, whiskey cupcakes always get them.

My mom's peanut butter pie tastes like home. It's rich but not too heavy. It reminds you a little bit of peanut butter sandwiches, and it takes you to that place where you're young and hungry and that first bite of peanut butter's the best taste in the world.

It's a Lambert family classic. Anytime it's served is good, but it is absolutely *the* required follow-up to the Loaf, especially if you're making it to get "a ring on it." You have to finish that meal with the peanut butter pie, no questions asked.

Mom jokes that you shouldn't make this meal if you're not sure about wanting that ring, because once someone has the Loaf, mashed potatoes, green beans, and yeast rolls, finished off with her peanut butter pie, they're a goner. If you want someone to close their eyes and think of the home they want to create with someone they love—even a home they never had—this is the meal that closes the deal. Peanut butter pie isn't just for making things "official," though; it's for anytime you want someone to know they're loved or feel like they're "home."

When a dish makes you think of a certain person, it makes dessert a little more special—and sweeter too. Of course, you love the flavors, but there's something more.

Cherry salad is one of those dishes. It's a very confusing thing, as it was usually served as a side dish, not a dessert. It is cold and sweet-tart, and so creamy it melts in your mouth. There's nothing complicated about it, no secret ingredient that makes it delicious. It's something anyone can make, but my mom made it for us. Anytime we'd go somewhere—for a party or a potluck—people would request it. It's not too sweet, but it's absolutely, exactly *her*. When I was young, I thought of it like "pre-dessert," a little taste of what was to come. Plus, even if I didn't finish my dinner, I'd already had my dessert. But part of me feels like we should get real and call it a dessert, period. That's what it's all about—not what you call it, but what you think when you eat it. To this day, when I close my eyes, no matter where I am, I can still taste it. When a dish can take you away like that, you know it's something special—and it can be a salad, a dessert, or a pre-dessert without changing a single ingredient.

Hummingbird CAKE

SERVES 8 TO 10

CAKE

Cooking spray

3 cups all-purpose flour, plus more for dusting

1½ cups chopped pecans

2 cups granulated sugar

1 teaspoon baking soda

1 teaspoon ground cinnamon

½ teaspoon salt

3 large eggs, lightly beaten

1¾ cups mashed ripe banana (from about 4 large bananas)

1 (8-ounce) can crushed pineapple with juices

¾ cup canola oil

1½ teaspoons vanilla extract

GLAZE

4 ounces cream cheese, cubed and softened

2 cups powdered sugar

1 to 2 tablespoons whole milk

1 teaspoon vanilla extract

MAKE the cake: Preheat the oven to 350°F. Grease a 14-cup Bundt pan with cooking spray and dust with flour.

ADD the pecans in a single layer to a shallow baking pan and bake for 8 to 10 minutes, until toasted and fragrant, stirring halfway through.

IN a large bowl, stir together the flour, granulated sugar, baking soda, cinnamon, and salt. Add the eggs, bananas, pineapple, oil, and vanilla. Stir just until the dry ingredients are moistened.

SPRINKLE 1 cup of the toasted pecans into the prepared Bundt pan. Spoon the batter over the pecans. Bake for 60 to 70 minutes, until a toothpick inserted in the center comes out clean.

WHILE the cake bakes, make the glaze: In a bowl, stir together the cream cheese, powdered sugar, milk, and vanilla until smooth.

LET the cake cool in the pan for 15 minutes, then transfer to a wire rack. Let cool for another 15 minutes, then brush on the glaze. Let sit for at least 1 hour before serving.

Rum BALLS

MAKES ABOUT 28

1 (11-ounce) box Nilla Wafers

2 cups powdered sugar, plus more for rolling

1 cup chopped pecans, plus more for rolling

¼ cup unsweetened cocoa

4 ounces (½ cup) rum

3 tablespoons dark corn syrup

PULSE the cookies in a food processor until broken up (about 10 pulses). Add the powdered sugar, pecans, cocoa, rum, and corn syrup and pulse until beginning to combine into one big ball.

SHAPE into 1-inch balls and roll in additional powdered sugar and chopped pecans. Store the rum balls in an airtight container in the refrigerator for up to 2 weeks or in the freezer for up to 2 months. Allow to come to room temperature before serving.

Whiskey CUPCAKES

MAKES 18 CUPCAKES

Cooking spray

1 (8-ounce) package cream cheese, softened

1 large egg, slightly beaten

1⅓ cups sugar

½ teaspoon salt

1¼ cups semisweet mini chocolate chips

1½ cups all-purpose flour

¼ cup unsweetened cocoa

1 teaspoon ground cinnamon

1 teaspoon baking soda

2 ounces (¼ cup) whiskey

¾ cup water

⅓ cup vegetable oil

1 tablespoon white vinegar

2 teaspoons vanilla extract

PREHEAT the oven to 350°F. Grease 18 muffin cups or use paper liners.

IN a large bowl, combine the cream cheese, egg, ⅓ cup of the sugar, and ¼ teaspoon of the salt. Stir in the chocolate chips and set aside.

IN another large bowl, combine the flour, remaining 1 cup sugar, the cocoa, cinnamon, baking soda, and remaining ¼ teaspoon salt. In a separate bowl, stir together the whiskey, water, oil, vinegar, and vanilla. Stir into the flour mixture until fully incorporated.

FILL each muffin cup three-quarters full with the cupcake batter. Add 1 tablespoon of the cream cheese mixture to the center of each cupcake.

BAKE for 35 to 40 minutes, until a toothpick inserted in the center comes out clean. Cool for 10 minutes in the pan. Transfer to a wire rack and let cool for 20 minutes.

Peanut Butter
PIE

SERVES 6 TO 8

1 (4.6-ounce) box vanilla pudding mix (I like Jell-O Vanilla Cook & Serve)

3 cups whole milk

1 cup crunchy peanut butter

1 prebaked 9-inch piecrust

1 (8-ounce) tub whipped topping, thawed if frozen (I like Cool Whip), or 2 cups Whipped Cream (recipe follows)

6 ounces slightly salted peanuts

COOK the pudding with the milk according to the package directions.

REMOVE the pudding from the heat, stir in the peanut butter, and let the mixture cool.

POUR the cooled filling into the piecrust. Refrigerate for 1 hour. The filling will not be firm, but should not be jiggly. Before serving, top with whipped topping and sprinkle with peanuts.

WHIPPED CREAM

2 cups heavy cream

1 tablespoon powdered sugar

IN a metal or glass bowl, whip the cream with the powdered sugar until firm. Chill and serve with pie.

Cherry SALAD

SERVES 6 TO 8

1 (12-ounce) can cherry pie filling

1 (14-ounce) can sweetened condensed milk (I like Eagle Brand)

1 (8-ounce) can crushed pineapple

1 (8-ounce) tub whipped topping, thawed if frozen (I like Cool Whip)

Whipped Cream (page 207) and fresh mint, for topping (optional)

IN a bowl, fold together the cherry pie filling, condensed milk, crushed pineapple, and whipped topping. Pour into a 9 x 11-inch casserole. Refrigerate for at least 6 hours or overnight.

IF desired, top with whipped cream and mint, if desired, before serving.

11

CELEBRATE!
CELEBRATE!
CELEBRATE!

▼▼▼▼▼▼▼▼▼▼▼▼▼▼▼▼▼▼

If there is one thing we in the (extended) Lambert house love, it's a party! And as much as we love to get together, laughing and playing music, that's just us being us. A party means a few extra things.

It's something to celebrate, of course. And just about *anything* can be celebrated. Whether it's a new job, a new puppy, a promotion, dumping a bad boyfriend, a baby going to kindergarten or college, a favorite band coming to town, or, well, any holiday, birthday, or my hair's cute today, you've got your reason.

We also love anything with a theme. Themes not only set the tone, but they also give you a reason and a way to really "apply yourself" to whatever this party's going to be. Whether it's how we decorate, what we cook, or what we wear, those themes add a whole other layer of fun—and sometimes games—to what we're doing.

Then it's making sure you've got all the people you love sharing the moment with you. Sometimes a party is for just a few, but sometimes it's for a whole lot of people. If it's gonna be a big one, then figuring out how to make it easy so you can enjoy all those guests is the name of the game.

Mom, Nonny, and everyone who's part of our crew are party ninjas. Here are just a few of our most favorite parties, memories, and ideas.

BIRTHDAYS

Birthdays for us were—*surprise*—a big deal. My mom made sure the cupcakes got to our classrooms, of course, but it was the way she celebrated our birthdays when Luke and I got home from school that really mattered. It always started when she came to pick us up with the balloons hanging off the car, just flying in the wind like absolute freedom when she drove up.

My mom *knows* how to throw a party. So did Nonny. For them, it was about fun, of course, but also about making memories. Funny thing is, it was never about spending a ton of money on a bounce house or six kinds of fancy food trucks. It was always more about knowing who was coming, then doing something that'd rock their worlds.

Case in point: my tenth birthday party. My mom thought double digits was a really, *really* big deal. When I turned ten, it wasn't that classic big-deal party with a bunch of kids at Chuck E. Cheese, or getting a magician or a pony—because, honestly, any kid where we lived who wanted a pony had one—but something *truly* Bev Lambert spectacular.

As only she could, because my parents knew how much I loved music, Mom found a way to make music a massive part of how we celebrated.

Bev Lambert actually booked the local rodeo arena and threw a party for 120 people! It was one of the biggest events that year, and it was crazy fun. Everybody came, everybody had a blast. My parents borrowed a flatbed trailer, which was rolled out into the ring, where my dad played an entire honky-tonk set! He just got out there and wailed, playing all the songs that made a Friday or Saturday night come alive. To me, it was like having George Strait or the Rolling Stones, only better, because it was *my* daddy.

Confederate Railroad's song "Trashy Women," written by a Texas artist named Chris Wall, was a big ol' hit around that time. Keeping that song in mind, my crazy mom figured out her own special way to "jump out of a cake," so to speak. She and the mother of the friend I wrote "Famous in a Small Town" about dressed up, literally, like "trashy" women; they totally went for it with the big hair and jacked-up everything. Then, when the band launched into that one special number, Mom and her friend got up on stage—padded bras, skintight pants, loud makeup, *everything* "Trashy Women" was about—and danced with zero shame, having entirely too much fun. The crowd went wild.

Being ten and not entirely used to this kind of energy, I was sort of humiliated and totally in awe *all* at the same time. You know, my mom having the nerve to just go full-on like that said a lot about the kind of stock I come from. Nothing comes between any of us and having the best time, and she knew—in a way I couldn't at that age—that people would find it absolutely hilarious to see someone they know throw down that kind of saucy humor.

Talk about a birthday gift that didn't come in a box with a bow on top. I felt so alive that night, I can't tell you. It was sorta silly and sorta awesome. And watching my dad and his friends play country music like that? It told me that even when you're not Willie Nelson or Dolly Parton, that music—when it's played with a lot of heart and passion—moves people right where they live. That was another amazing and meaningful gift.

Obviously, not every birthday party was such a big deal. A lot of times, it was just us at home. Mom would make whatever we wanted for dinner—almost every year, it was the Loaf—and our friends would come over. It was super easy and super comfortable, but also exactly what each of us really wanted. Sometimes just being with your friends, laughing, and eating your favorite meal is the perfect way to enjoy turning a year older.

When I turned sixteen, we had a bonfire for all my friends, just this massive fire where we all stood around roasting wienies on sticks, laughing, and having the best time. To me, that's the magic: when you can make something out of nothing and just have fun with your people. Parties don't have to be this massive "thing" that takes so much work, you're actually exhausted by the time you're there. Where's the fun in that?

My Sweet 16, if you call it that, was all about chili dogs and Frito pie, which may sound very exotic to some people. Frito pie is just a grab 'n' go way to eat chili! You slice open a bag of corn chips, right down the middle like you would a baked potato. Then you scoop your chili into that hole, add jalapeños, onions, sour cream, whatever you like—and grab a fork. It's the simplest trick, but you can hold it in your hand, mix it up, and let it get all melty and delicious. Then you can walk around with it and see what's going on while enjoying your snack. *And* it sticks to your ribs. Maybe it's just one of those Texas things, but it's one of those Texas things that makes me glad I'm a Texas girl.

And—surprise—my dad played music. I can't tell you how many parties my dad would have his guitar out sharing music with us, from when I was so tiny I'd be sleeping in his lap while he played right straight through to when I was a teenager. He was always ready to play and knew how to keep the party going with the songs he chose; he knew what people liked—and he knew how to put a song across with a real sense of not just rhythm, but also the feeling inside.

For me the fun is in the people. The reason you're getting together is more of an excuse maybe, but who cares? I've been to all kinds of parties, but it always comes down to who's there. Case in point: when I turned twenty-one, I spent my birthday with my mom, Nonny, and her friends. Of course I did. First, we had a huge yard party with a flatbed, a sound system, and lights strung across the front pasture. We had a full-on barbecue dinner for around one hundred people. That was just the warm-up! The next day I left with the Ya-Yas and Mom.

Let me point out: Nonny was a big-time small-time gambler. It wasn't that she was throwing around hundred-dollar bills or playing at the thousand-dollar tables, but she played *a lot*. Every dealer, every waitress, every hotel

and casino manager *knew* Nonny; she was a regular customer and a whole lot of fun when she was playing. Also, she loved all those people, and they loved her.

For my twenty-first birthday, a casino actually sent a limousine from Shreveport and comped Nonny two rooms. So we got in that long white stretch with the tan vinyl top and steered toward "the boat." We were headed for Harrah's with a vengeance. In Louisiana, the gambling's actually on the water. I'm not sure how they get away with it, but it makes gambling legal— and creates a connection to those old Southern riverboat adventures.

When we got there, they rolled out the carpet for us! It was "Mrs. Coker's granddaughter's twenty-first!"—and everyone made us feel special with drinks and what have you. When you're young, that kind of thing feels like a *big* deal. Even when you've been singing your songs in bars for years, trust me, this was "glamorous."

I remember I was in a Bacardí and Coke phase. Talk about young and not knowing better! I thought they were just the best thing ever, because I was all of twenty-one and they seemed fancy. We stayed out too late, drank too much, laughed too loud. What one of those women didn't think up, someone else did, said, or joked about.

Nonny only played quarter slots. She was smart about her money, maybe even a little frugal. She only gambled with her allowance from Pop-Pop, which was $1,200. She knew how to make that money last. Sometimes she won pretty big, and Pop-Pop *never* asked her to share her winnings or even pay back her "stake."

She'd get all dressed up in her rhinestones, looking flashy. She used to wear her real diamonds, but Mom didn't like that one bit. Being a detective, Mom knew all that flash might attract the wrong kinds of people. Nonny would just laugh and say, "You gotta get your diamonds on and sparkle for the machines!" That's how she got lucky! She'd get all fancied up, put on her bling, and go down to the casino. Nonny even had this crazy nugget ring with a giant rhinestone "7," because it's such a lucky number. She used to tell me, "You have to excite the machines!" Boy, did she. She'd come along shining like a diamond, and you just felt lucky standing next to her.

That was a birthday. Another birthday of a lifetime. Nonny, her entire pack of granny friends, Mom, and me. Who better to turn twenty-one with than a bunch of seventy-year-old ladies who knew how to live out loud and fabulous?

How could you top that? You can't. You shouldn't even try.

When I turned twenty-two, in 2005, the 39th Annual Country Music Association Awards went to New York City. It was a big deal, and Manhattan really turned out for the event. There were flags on the streetlights and a buzz in the air. All the country stars were staying in town, running around, and enjoying New York. There were parties everywhere and entirely too much to do.

I had been nominated for the Horizon Award, which is now called New Artist of the Year. It was a big deal, because I was going against the grain. I wanted to write my songs and sound fiercer than many of the other female artists.

When we negotiated my record deal, that was one thing I was sure of. I *knew* I didn't just want a record deal; I wanted one where I could make my music my way. I was told it might take longer or not work out at all, but I figured I'd rather do the work for my music than chase what someone thought I should be doing. So that nomination was big, especially for all the other girls who didn't want to just be what they were told to be.

The awards were held at Madison Square Garden; Brooks & Dunn hosted. But the big news—besides my birthday that trip—was that I was booked to perform "Kerosene." A little thrashing rock-country seems like a good idea, right?

My actual birthday was two nights before the show, so we decided to find a place that was true to who we are. We found the only real country dive bar in New York City: Doc Holliday's, which is way *downtown*. We're talking Ave A and 9th Street, pretty much the last place you'd expect an actual ride-or-die honky-tonk beer joint.

But if you know anything about real-life honky-tonk beer joints, that's *exactly* the place you'd find one! A little bit biker-bar vibe, a pool table, beer in cans, women bartenders with attitude, tiny lights hung from the ceiling, and an honest-to-God jukebox-stacked-with-vinyl kind of place? That was Doc Holliday's. Cash only, don't lip the staff, and get ready to dance on the bar!

We hit that place like it was the last beer joint in New York City—it was Mom, Heidi and Vicki, and a bunch of friends and country artists who will remain anonymous under the "code of the road." Doc's is open from noon 'til 4 a.m., and let's just say we kept rolling. We played so much Merle Haggard, Willie Nelson, Steve Earle, Emmylou Harris, and George Strait, you would've thought we were back home in Texas. The dress code was country-and-western *only*. Every single person wore fringe, pearl snaps, and boots. We were amongst "our kind."

It was nothing like turning twenty-one, but it was every bit as awesome. Sometimes you can take the girl out of Texas but still bring Texas—or wherever you love—right along with you.

Since Mom, Dad, Heidi, and Vicki had all flown in for my birthday, and we couldn't get them tickets to the show, they just went back to Doc's. It was a big night for *all* of us, and making friends like they do, where could be better?

"Kerosene," you have to understand, was too long a song for a young new artist to play *all* of, so we made an edit. Then, because it was TV, they wanted to flash everything up. Well, with me, with *this* song, what better reason for the producers to call in pyro? They wanted an actual wall of flames to be shooting up between me and the band.

Those shows can seem really tedious when you're sitting there watching, but there's a lot of rushing around backstage. Sets rolling on and off, musicians being slammed into place, quick cues and—BOOM!—you're on.

Never mind all the different cameras and people cuing other segments coming up. The light hits and you play. You play for all you're worth, especially when you're a young act and you're not the reason people are tuning in.

So we hit it, hard. But then there was that edit. And that wall of fire was costing $40,000—and I had to pay it back somehow. In all the rush, I got confused. I didn't know if I'd missed the edit; where I'd normally look back at the band and they'd nod that it was all cool—WHOOSH!—the flames shot up.

I didn't know what to do, so I started this wild, crazy dancing. I figured, "Go full Stevie Nicks!" Just stomp and spin; if I screwed up the lyrics, nobody would notice. That stuff blurs, honestly. But I do remember Lee Ann Womack, who is a big hero of mine. She half-jokingly told her husband, Frank Liddell, who is my producer, to go apologize to my whole family, because he'd ruined my career. But after she heard "Kerosene" all the way through, she was standing there, on her feet, giving me the biggest standing ovation.

When I finally got offstage, out of breath, the first thing I did was call my mom.

"Oh, my God, I just ruined my career," I yelped into the phone.

"Are you kidding? You killed it! Oh, my God, Miranda, you won the whole thing."

I didn't know. But see, that's the beauty of how I was raised. Win or lose, you're in a honky-tonk in the Village where the drinks are $4 and the jukebox is hard country. That's a big yes! Not to mention, everyone you know is there celebrating the moment.

Turned out Mom was right. People loved the performance and said I was the breakout star of the night! It was once again the best birthday present I could've had—and it was a rager of a party even though I didn't get there until after we did all the interviews and "official" parties. They were still going, and I was ready. Nothing fancy, just loud, proud, and getting down with people who liked to celebrate the same way we do.

WHITE TRASH WEDDINGS AND BABY SHOWERS

Okay, let's get real. We've all seen those lovely, Instagram-perfect showers where everything is just so very . . . perfect. The napkins are monogrammed; there are miniature macarons that match the color palette. Every single thing is so pretty, it's hard to imagine taking a bite, let alone letting down your hair or having fun.

To me, the more creative, the more ironic, the more kick-off-your-shoes-and-make-yourself-comfortable, the better. Especially when it's one of those events that're as much made up as an excuse to have a party as they are following any real established tradition. Wedding showers are as much an excuse to celebrate someone you love who's about to do something life-changing and, theorctically, wonderful as they are about buying things for their kitchen and getting too drunk on whatever their squad is into that year.

You can have little quiche and those pastel-colored almonds in the tiny paper cups, if that's what you like. I think to each her own. But when you're talking to us—Mama, the Ya-Yas, Nonny, her crew, or my friends—we're always going to go for mixing it up, maybe even shaking it up. Let's face it: you can take the redneck out of the pictures, but you're not taking the white trash out of the girl. Rub any single one of us just a little the wrong way, you'll see. Why not give in to your untamed white-trash super hussy? Vamp it up, ramp it up, and camp it up, I say! It's not every day you can really get your trailer park swerve on, so grab the opportunity with both hands. This is the part where the tacky gets to come out in good fun among good friends.

It's easy. It's hilarious. It's a mandate to give in to your wilder side.

When I got married for the first time, Beverly Lambert knew the last thing we needed was some great big fancy to-do. I was never one of those girls who lies awake at night dreaming of getting married and riding off into the sunset; I was more the kind to dream about writing songs, floating the river with my friends, winning Entertainer of the Year.

So, to be real *and* to celebrate, my mom, the same woman who threw a great big honky-tonk show and chili cook-off for my tenth birthday, figured, "Let's let our roots show." And she meant the roots on our heads, for our friends who aren't blessed with naturally blond hair. Be just as fun and outrageous and playing to stereotypes as we please. There's a lot of fun in letting your hair down and playing with the over-the-top clichés. Why not jack up your hair? How high? Is that all? Maybe add a flower, a tiara. Go on. Pick out your favorite leopard print. ALL OVER. Mix 'n' match colors, or animals. Electric neon. Pink and black. Just do it.

Break out a new (temporary or not) tattoo. Make sure the spelling's right. We had a really good friend, a pretty dignified and very well-respected nurse practitioner, who arrived in a cutoff T-shirt with a temporary tat that read "Hit It & Quit It" just above her bikini line.

That's the whole point of the (White) Trashy-Ho Wedding Shower: turn all the traditions on their head, maybe play against type. Set your inner wild thing loose, then laugh until your sides hurt.

Not to mention, the best part of a trashy-ho shower is *really* letting your metaphorical hair down too—and letting it all hang out. Be as loud as you want! The music. The clothes. Your voice. In fact, if you're not whooping and hollering pretty loud—and laughing even louder—you may not be trashy enough.

When we did my shower, it was at Mom's house in Texas. She has a little cantina in the back that's equal parts cantina and tiki bar—because why be just one thing when you can be both? See what I mean about go big or go crazy? Anything's possible when we set to dreaming up without limits.

Mom's cantina is outdoors, so we could be in nature while wearing crazy, tacky, fun—in my case, a wig with shiny, long bright red hair things. That contrast becomes even more so "in the wild." She always has the cantina all strung up with little lights, so it's twinkly every night. But add lots of Solo cups in all kinds of colors, floozie koozies for the "canned beverages," and lots of ice tubs everywhere, and you're talking next-level.

This definitely wasn't debutante stuff, but everything about it said, "Come on! Kick off your shoes *or* leave your stilettos on—and get in here! Get something to drink and start laughing your ass off."

Mom's current place definitely exists as party ready. But even when we had the small house with the tiny kitchen, she made any kind of party that came to her mind work.

Take that to heart. Know, truly, that any backyard—or front yard, if you don't care what the neighbors think!—will do. Get yourself a little kiddie pool and a hose, some pink flamingos (*lots* of pink flamingos). Some boas are a nice touch. And stringing up those little lights will turn *any* space into a beer garden. To me, it's all about taking the pressure off. You're getting together with your besties, or in my case, my besties, my mom's besties, and any like-minded tagalongs, 'cause that's where the best "new" besties come from!

Everybody told crazy stories at my shower. Neicy's brother Zack catered it. There were little shot glasses of grits with one tiny shrimp on top, mini sloppy joes, Jell-O shots. He set up stations for Tex-Mex, home cookin', and Cajun, with shots to complement all of them. The home-cookin' station was the introduction of the Potini Bar (page 230), with brisket, fried chicken, gravy, cheese dip, sour cream, caramelized onions, chives, and bacon.

Knowing our squad by now, you know folks brought *all* the dips, and Heidi's cheese ball and Heidi's hot crackers. Our friends just can't help themselves! We had vegetable trays, corn chips for dipping; cold beer, chilled wine, and plenty of tequila, vodka, and whiskey to drink. There was even a champagne fountain with flutes as well as a milk fountain with a cookie river. Even a crazy wedding shower is pretty much built on *all* the regular doings, just with a little extra—and a twist.

And that twist—"what's your trashy-ho look?"—makes for the extra fun, partially because in the days before the party, it gives you so much to talk about. People were coming up with their outfits, checking in with each other, deciding what sort of trashy ho they wanted to be. There are all kinds, you know, and it's not a choice to be taken lightly. I laughed listening to it all. The level of thought that went into some of these outfits, the idea of who was going to be the trashiest of them all, it was too much. When you give our friends permission, they're all absolutely and completely shameless!

Somebody—okay, Neicy—showed up at my place in a cutoff Hooters T-shirt with these fake boobs actually hanging out of the bottom of the shirt. When anyone saw her, they couldn't stop laughing, because we've all seen this at some sports bar, and elbowed each other and eye-rolled about the girl thinking she's all that. But, here at my mama's cantina, Neicy had it on strut like a peacock.

That's part of what I love about this group of women: no shame, all game. Once everybody got there, we started celebrating. My mom had already decided that before things started we had to have a fashion show. People had put good work into their "looks," so everybody needed to *strut*. And that's what we did. We had a very fancy fashion show of our outrageous looks: the shortest miniskirt, the most pushed-up bra, the biggest beehive, the tallest heels. People, especially the girls who are sometimes the quiet ones, were so proud of what they pulled off! And they should've been. We even had Nonny in her pink-and-black feather boa leading the parade as we laughed and stomped through "the show." We were just snaking around like a big old Technicolor conga line.

Those are the memories money can't buy. Sure, you could spend a fortune, but I promise: you won't look back on an event like that with more joy or more laughter (even now) than we do when we think about our "let-your-inner-ho-go-wild" shower. Don't worry so much about what kind of wineglasses, or how much money you're spending on the food. Do something unexpected people will talk about for years. Come up with a great idea, a crazy notion that will capture people's hearts and imaginations. It will also make for stories they'll all tell for years.

And that's not just true for weddings. This concept works great for, well, pretty much anything! When Ashley Monroe got pregnant, there was only one way to celebrate. White Trash Baby Shower! We got together and threw her the biggest Pistol Annies'–style trailer park kinda shower we could imagine! We had chicken and dressing, barbecue, banana pudding. When I think of Ashley, I think of *all* things that are down-home and Southern. It's not just the food either, but the heart. She has a very special kind of heart: a little hippie, a little wild, a little bit silk, and as big as the Smoky Mountains of East Tennessee. When I was trying to figure out what kind of baby shower to do for her, I realized all I needed was to go back to her roots. If you've ever listened to one of our Pistol Annies' records, you already know— Ashley savors the outrageous extremes every bit as much as we do.

Like Mom did for my wedding shower, I did it all at my farmhouse. There's something about keeping the party at home that sets a tone of welcome, of anything goes, but also keeps it safe. We made everybody comfortable, set dips all over, and turned up the music.

For vibe, we played to what we had—and what would be hilarious. We went to the toy store and found rubber ducks that little kids would use in the bathtub; I think we bought every single one. When people walked out into the backyard, they saw this whole flock of rubber baby ducklings in the pool; we let them just float. It wasn't really nursery or Mother Goosey, but it had that sense of babies, trailers, and fun. We had washtubs of ice everywhere with all kinds of longnecks and cans sticking out. We had drinks in mason jars. It didn't matter what you were having, it was like being in a honky-tonk in the woods with a bunch of girls having the time of their lives celebrating a brand-new life in the making.

We even got together a very special kind of cornhole. Not everyone knows the game, but if you do, you can imagine why we called it "sperm in the hole." Beyond! Two wood boards, all of us pitching beanbags at a six-inch hole, nine inches from the top and twelve inches from either side. The cornhole bags were covered in white fabric with rubber band tails hanging down. We drew baby faces on them with Sharpies. Mom still has them! It sounds easy, 'til you add beer, wine, or gin, or any such combination. The opportunity for jokes when you're taking aim is truly endless. And every time someone got their bag to drop inside the hole, we'd all scream like it was spring break. Dumb. Fun. But that's the point of a trashy anything: celebrate that side because it's silly, not serious. Remember: the whole idea is to take that "preacher is coming over" pressure off.

POTINI BARS AND OTHER THEMES

When you love to entertain—or, really, just to have people over—as much as every single one of us does, you learn to make things easy on yourself. Yes, I love making a Hummingbird Cake when I'm going to someone's house, because it looks fancy and all, but I'd rather have more fun and less fuss.

Nobody understood that concept more than Mom and Nonny, who'd have all her friends out on the back patio smoking cigarettes, drinking Canadian Hunter, and working on a cheese ball. But my mom, who worked pretty long and odd hours when my parents were on a case, never wanted to let work get in the way of having fun or fellowship—and, trust me, she didn't. My parents could throw chicken and sausage on the grill, ice down some beers, and have a party started in a matter of minutes; add Dad's guitar, and we could go all night. After all, you never run out of songs you love or stories to tell. Along the way, Mom came up with a couple tricks that are so ingenious, I think everybody should be in on the secret. While her chicken salad, deviled eggs and the Loaf are the perennials, her take on Zack's "potini bar" may be the most universal crowd-pleaser of all. How do you go wrong with mashed potatoes or delicious things to put on top of them? Exactly. Plus, you get to make a DIY dinner that seems both a little fancy and completely unexpected. If you use Mom's guaranteed-to-please second course—dessert made from mashed sweet potatoes—you'll have exactly *one* dish to clean up.

I'm ahead of myself, but potini bars tend to do this to me. So let's break this down. A potini bar is where a scoop of mashed potatoes is put into a martini glass, then each person selects from all different kinds of toppings. There are always meat toppings, sometimes someone'll bring barbecue, and Mom might make taco meat, chili, or even fried chicken. On those occasions when we're very lucky, Neicy will bring gumbo.

After you choose your protein, you head over to all the other goodies. Avocados or guac, salsa or bits of tomatoes, all different kinds of jalapeños and hot peppers, shredded lettuce. We might have sour cream, queso, or shredded cheddar cheese, and three different kinds of salsa. Depending on the meat, there might be pickles, coleslaw, gravy, hot vinegar with the peppers in it. Go wild! You know your guests. If it's a really big party, you can set up a nacho bar too. You've got everything you need.

With a potini bar, everyone gets to make their dinner exactly how they like it, which means everyone's meal is perfect. Once again, people are part of putting the dinner together, an activity that's as much fun as actually eating it all up. When everybody's finished, they move on to the sweet course! My mom has a sink in her cantina to rinse the glasses, but you can set up a pitcher of water to rinse, with a tub to dump the water when you're done.

Next, out comes a giant tub of the fluffiest whipped sweet potatoes. Once you get your scoop, you can start on the toppings. There are marshmallows, marshmallow sauce, coconut, pecans, walnuts, pralines broken into bits, brown sugar, maple syrup, cinnamon, sprinkles, and pieces of pretzel for people who like the salty with their sweet. How easy is that? One glass, one fork, one spoon, and one napkin—okay, maybe two.

When the meal is over, load everything into the dishwasher and you're done. With a big group of people, there's usually very little left over. If there is, you can send people home with "go" cups for the road. This meal is just as good the next day, though I think most people don't get anywhere near home before they've eaten their leftover portion too.

Mom does this so often, she has her own set of oversize acrylic martini glasses in all different colors. She loves the way they slant in because people load up their "plates" without having stuff slop over the side. Her glasses have hollow stems. I guess if you're drinking, that means even more martini for you, but Mom takes that hollow stem and puts it to work. She'll drop an olive, cherry tomato, tiny pickle, or jalapeño into it to keep the potatoes and fixings from getting down where it's hard to clean and impossible to eat. It looks cute and reinforces the evening's theme.

There's also a bonus bar possibility. Nobody does a DIY mimosa bar like we do. Get a few fresh fruit juices, some cordials, strawberries or little fruit skewers for the rim. Just like that, you're fancy.

Where we really excel, though, is with a Bloody Mary bar. We make our mix in regular, spicy, and extra spicy, then line up a big mess of goodness to put on skewers. You have to decide if you want a celery stick stirrer, or a skewer with olives and onions and pickles, maybe a little nibble of venison sausage, a chunk of cheese, a candied bacon stick, or a skewer of shrimp. Top it all with your choice of hot sauce. Bloody Mary perfection.

Themes are big in our group. We love a concept to pull the party together. Mom jokes about making her cantina an equal-opportunity tiki bar, a place where "everybody can get lei'd." Some of our best parties have been Polynesian-themed. Mom loves a luau. When you put a pig on a spit and roast it until it's perfectly cooked, there's nothing like it. The barbecue men in our extended tribe, they live for that stuff. We also live for rum drinks in pineapples, fruit salad, treats sprinkled with coconut, and anything with parasols. Plus, putting on Hawaiian shirts, sarongs, and tropical dresses is just one more way to beat the Texas heat. It's a long way to the big island of Honolulu, but if the tiny lights are right—and if my dad sings some Marty Robbins—it's Honolulu, Texas, in our backyard.

Let's be real: Life can be hard. Work can drag you down. Nightlife can bore you. We figure that every party, no matter the occasion, is the perfect chance to take a vacation from the stress of life.

BBQ MEATBALLS

1 pound ground beef, preferably ground round

1 pound ground pork sausage (I like Jimmy Dean)

1 (18-ounce) bottle barbecue sauce (I like Kraft Original)

MIX the ground beef and sausage together by hand. Shape into 1-inch balls. Cook in a skillet over medium heat for 30 to 45 minutes, until the meatballs are browned and slightly crispy. Drain off the fat, then pour in the barbecue sauce to cover the meatballs. Let simmer for another 30 minutes to incorporate the flavors before serving.

Easy
FRUIT SALAD

SERVES 6 TO 8

1 (15-ounce) can sliced pears, drained

1 (15-ounce) can sliced peaches, drained

1 (8-ounce) can pineapple tidbits, drained

1 (8.25-ounce) can mandarin oranges, drained

1 (14-ounce) bag frozen sliced strawberries

IN a large bowl, mix together the pears, peaches, pineapple, and oranges. Add the strawberries on top. When the strawberries have thawed and their juices have mixed through the rest of the fruit, gently stir again and serve.

POTINI BAR
SUPER-EASY MASHED POTATOES

SERVES 6

3 pounds potatoes, peeled and diced

Kosher salt

1 cup (2 sticks) unsalted butter

½ to ¾ cup heavy cream

Freshly ground black pepper

ADD the potatoes to a pot of cold salted water. Bring to a boil over high heat. Reduce the heat and simmer until fork-tender, about 20 minutes. Drain the potatoes. Return to the pot over medium-low heat. Cook, stirring, for 2 to 3 minutes, until the liquid has evaporated. Turn off the heat. Mash the potatoes with a potato masher to your desired consistency. Add the butter and heavy cream and stir until smooth. Season with salt and pepper.

MASHED SWEET POTATOES

SERVES 6

4 pounds sweet potatoes, peeled and cut into 2-inch chunks

Kosher salt

½ cup (1 stick) unsalted butter

⅓ cup heavy cream

¼ teaspoon ground cinnamon

Freshly ground black pepper

Fresh herbs, for garnish

ADD the potatoes to a pot of cold salted water. Bring to a boil over high heat. Reduce the heat to low and simmer until fork-tender, about 20 minutes. Drain the potatoes and transfer to a large bowl. Let sit for 5 to 10 minutes. Add the butter and mash the sweet potatoes with a potato masher to your desired consistency. Mix in the heavy cream, cinnamon, and salt and pepper to taste. Garnish with fresh herbs.

Potini
TOPPINGS

HOT/WARM TOPPINGS

BBQ brisket

Fried chicken

Sloppy Joes

Pulled roasted chicken

Chili

Gumbo

Queso

CHEESE + SAUCES

Grated cheddar cheese

Shredded Monterey Jack

Crumbled blue cheese

Cotija cheese

Sour cream

Guacamole

Green, red, or fresca salsa

BBQ sauce

Tabasco or hot sauce

VEGETABLES

Shredded lettuce

Diced tomatoes

Diced, sliced, or cubed fresh
red or green peppers

Minced onions

Green onions

Crushed onion rings

Jalapeños

SWEET POTINI TOPPINGS

Candied pecans or pralines

Chopped nuts

Spiced almonds

Mini marshmallows

Shredded coconut

Pretzel pieces

Chocolate chips

SAUCES + DUSTINGS

Marshmallow sauce

Caramel sauce

**Maple syrup or maple syrup
with bourbon**

**Brown sugar, cinnamon, or
powdered sugar**

FOOD DOESN'T FIX EVERYTHING

▼▼▼▼▼▼▼▼▼▼▼▼▼▼▼▼▼▼▼

Breakfast and Bad News

"What do you do with the diamonds?"

Friendships are only as strong as how well they weather the big stuff. Good news—engagements, weddings, babies, promotions—and the stuff nobody wants to deal with—death, major illness, divorce, losing a job—define people, but those things also reveal who your friends truly are. The people who go through the lows with you, who understand and help you through those times, are the ones who genuinely understand why the highs are so special.

With all these women, because every one of us lives life full-on and with our hearts wide open, there might be more highs and lows than the average. Sometimes I think we're bolder and braver, maybe even fearless, because we *all* know we've got backup in the form of these badass women who get things done.

Mom and her friends are especially great when things fall apart. These women close ranks like nobody you've ever seen. They're the "closing-est of rank closers," Mom says. We obviously love a party. They're great. When you're falling through space, waiting to splatter, or are already in pieces on the ground, sometimes there's nothing better than tying one on. If that's what you need, we got you—but the real stuff, the healing and the helping, comes out in the morning.

There's never any judgment with this crowd. Even if you did the most terrible thing, there is absolutely *no* judgment against you. You better be ready, though, because things will get real, real fast. Maybe it grew out of the core group always staying over, always staying the weekend. The last ones standing but also the first ones up in the morning with the coffee— those are the friends who match you moment to moment.

That knowing when and where, being there, is a gift.

When stuff starts going south, it seems like everybody just shows up. They know. When Rod's health started to fail, it was a major event for all of us. He'd been Dad's best friend since they were five; he and Neicy were almost our spare parents.

When Rod got sick, it was about packing as much goodness and light into the days he had. He'd been sick for a long time, and you think you're prepared, but you're not. During that time, everyone promised Rod they were going to take care of Neicy, but how do you fill that kind of hole? How do you heal a loss that's really an amputation?

As soon as the news hit that Rod had passed away, everyone rallied. Over the next few months, they brought covered dishes and Kleenex, hugged Denise and the kids. Once the hoopla died down, the question was how to keep Neicy's head above water. My mom, Vicki, and Heidi took her trout fishing, one of the things on her bucket list. She came out to some shows. She was always with one of us. We tried to think about the things nobody else was thinking about.

And there was what this group does best of all: the coffee klatching. It sounds cute and all, but that's where the real conversations go down. Breakfast can be so much more than a meal or even the start to the day. When we're together, we always eat breakfast at the house, no matter where we may be.

We never go out for breakfast for a very specific reason: so we can start the day by checking in with each other. After waking up, it puts us all on the same track for the day—and, honestly, the jokes over whatever we might have happening—or happened the night before—get us started on the right note. We're doing so much more than having the first food of the day. In those times, we want to make sure no one's life gets left behind.

We eat a lot of breakfast. Heidi's lemon-blueberry muffins come in especially handy at times like these. They're a little bit sweet and a little bit tart, just like those moments we sometimes find ourselves in. Bacon, eggs, toast, or a breakfast casserole become a lot more than food when life's tough. Big conversations happen easier in the kitchen; they're about the sorts of topics you want to face with a clear head and a cup of coffee.

I remember Mom saying they were asking Neicy, "Are you going to sell the house?" and "Do you need a Realtor? Do you need us to come up to fix it up for showing?" Someone asked, "What about the insurance policy? Do you know where that is?"

These are not easy things to bring up or discuss, but they're exactly what you need to bring up in those times. You have to start to figure things out and face whatever is scaring you. It's your real friends who are going to wade in there with you, who see the horizon when you're just too overwhelmed to think about anything beyond the next breath. That's part of why those conversations won't happen at night. It's fine for something celebratory. That's what the night is for: celebrating life. But anything else? There are too many chances for talking over one another or shutting someone down who needs help when they're really struggling.

When we lost Nonny, it was the same way. Mom closed down. I don't have words for how I felt, because that was my nonny. Every one of the Ya-Yas came to our side, held us up when we were in grief for the piece of us that was gone. Like Neicy, we had time to get ready, but how do you say goodbye to the people who make such an impact on your whole life?

It was also the same when my divorce happened. April and Mom got in the truck and started driving to the house in Oklahoma. They packed it all up and headed straight to Nashville to move me into a new home. I was out on the road working because those shows booked months in advance don't stop just because somebody's life fell apart. That's when your deep peeps step in.

Over the years, we've all been through something: Vicki's house flooding; Rod's death; my divorce and the idea of *"Oh, God! Country music broke up,"* and everyone having a shit fit because two country singers got a divorce. It's not what you intended, but life happens. It's up to you what you do with it. Me? I choose Team Happiness every time. You get to choose how you're going to feel and respond. Why not take lemons and squeeze them in my drink? These women, and my girlfriends too, live by the same ideals.

Sometimes you've gotta look the happiest at the worst times. That's the reality. Even if someone's getting a divorce, the party must go on. It's probably healthy. Momentum helps you heal, and who wants to bring the people you love down? Nobody I know. It's the life preserver we all need when the shit hits the fan.

All my crew—and I hope your crew too—works on some very simple principles. When the moment is getting real, we don't want you to text; we want you to *talk* to us. Pick up the phone and let us hear your voice or, better yet, let's come together and feel that bond. There is nothing like a hug, a cup of coffee, and a forkful of Neicy's French toast casserole. It's amazing how powerful that is.

That's what we do, how we roll. For us, it's very much a reality of: cry, laugh, eat, drink, get it all out. Our group is about coping and dealing with the things you never want to think of so you can get back to higher ground. It's probably why we start at breakfast. The emotions—good, bad, or whatever—didn't matter as much as being together. Morning coffee's not just for the tough stuff, though. It's also where we laugh the most, acting out what happened from the night before, telling the same stories for the umpteenth time. We crack ourselves up around the breakfast table to start our day happy.

It's like the recipes in this book. Every one of them is home to me. They're hugs wrapped up in a lifetime of memories. Sometimes snacks aren't the answer, but they can serve as a pretty strong bridge to return to a place where you feel like yourself.

French Toast
CASEROLE

SERVES 6 TO 8

Unsalted butter, for greasing

1 loaf French bread

8 large eggs

2 cups whole milk

TOPPING

½ cup light brown sugar

½ cup all-purpose flour

1 teaspoon ground cinnamon

¼ teaspoon salt

½ cup heavy cream

½ cup sugar

½ cup light brown sugar

2 tablespoons vanilla extract

¼ pound (1 stick) unsalted butter

Syrup, powdered sugar, or fruit, for serving

PREHEAT the oven to 350°F. Grease an 8 x 8-inch casserole dish with butter.

TEAR the bread into chunks and place in the prepared dish. In a large bowl, whisk the eggs with the milk, heavy cream, both sugars, and the vanilla. Pour over the bread.

WHILE the bread soaks, make the topping: In a medium bowl, combine the brown sugar, flour, cinnamon, and salt. Add the butter and use a fork or pastry cutter to mix until crumbly.

SPRINKLE the topping over the bread mixture in the casserole dish. Bake for 45 to 55 minutes, until golden. To serve, top with syrup, powdered sugar, or fruit.

THE casserole can be assembled the night before without the topping and refrigerated until ready to bake the following morning. Let the casserole stand at room temperature for 15 to 20 minutes, then add the topping and bake.

Lemon-Blueberry MUFFINS

MAKES 1 DOZEN

Cooking spray

2 cups all-purpose flour

⅔ cup plus 1 tablespoon sugar

1 teaspoon baking powder

1 teaspoon baking soda

½ teaspoon salt

1 cup lemon-flavored yogurt

4 tablespoons (½ stick) unsalted butter, melted and cooled slightly

1 large egg, beaten

1 to 2 teaspoons lemon zest (from 1 lemon)

1 teaspoon vanilla extract

2 cups fresh or frozen blueberries

PREHEAT the oven to 400°F. Grease a 12-cup muffin tin with cooking spray with cooking spray or use paper liners.

IN a large bowl, stir together the flour, ⅔ cup sugar, the baking powder, baking soda, and salt. In another bowl, combine the yogurt, butter, egg, lemon zest, and vanilla until smooth. Make a well in the center of the dry ingredients and add the yogurt mixture. Stir just to combine. Stir in the blueberries.

SPOON the batter into the prepared muffin tin and sprinkle with the remaining 1 tablespoon sugar. Bake for 20 to 25 minutes, until a toothpick inserted in the center comes out clean. Let cool in the muffin tin for 5 minutes, then transfer to a wire rack to continue cooling. Serve the muffins warm or at room temperature.

Junk Gypsy Love

A family friend came upon the Junk Gypsies, Amie and Jolie Sikes, at an antique meet and said, "I think my friend would love your stuff." I'd just filmed *Nashville Star*, and it was starting to air. Even though I'd been playing around Texas, my friend never thought anyone would know who I was.

When Amie and Jolie pressed her, and she told them my name, they went, "We love her! We never missed an episode of the show. She just spoke to our hearts."

The Sikes sisters are from Northeast Texas like we are, so there's that connection, born in the dirt and the sky. You kind of "know" each other without ever meeting. But the Junk Gypsies are everything that I love and try to bring into my life: vintage, hippie, cowgirl-bohemian, eclectic rock-and-roll vibes that infuse everything they do and are.

Jolie likes to say, "We live the way we dress, and we dress the way we live."

Considering they started their business driving around in an old pickup truck, going to junk shops, flea markets, and yard sales, they sure do. Beyond the Junk-o-Rama Prom they started throwing in Round Top,

Texas, during Texas Antiques Week (which might be the most outrageously fun thing you'd never expect), they were getting started in their career around the same time I was.

Once I heard that they knew who I was, my mom jumped on the phone with them and started talking like she does. They were all besties after about the third back-and-forth and started talking about what I needed. I didn't have a logo, and we kind of knew that was going to be important.

While Jolie and Mom were laughing and cutting up on the phone, and Jolie was asking what I was like, Amie was sketching away! Before they even finished the conversation, Amie asked Jolie for our fax number. When Mom asked why, they told her they were gonna send us something. Whirrrrrr! Just like that, my logo came rolling off the fax machine: wings and two crossed pistols. Talk about the essence of who I am, especially back then! It was fantastic. Badass. Wild-hearted. Not afraid to fly. They nailed me!

They like to joke now that they sent the fax and then heard screaming. It scared them half to death, but that's how we live: out loud and full tilt.

When Mom asked how we could ever pay them, the girls just said, "You don't." Mom couldn't believe it. I'm not sure whether it was Jolie or Amie, but one of them said, "Just put our name on the back of those T-shirts. Say, 'Designed by the Junk Gypsies.'"

They say it's one of the smartest things they ever did. For me, having those girls believe in me at a time when things were starting to happen, when the world felt like everything's possible but could also just fall apart? This made me feel like the universe was with us.

What I wanted to do in country music was more aggressive and rawer than what was already happening. I wanted something that was still girlie and smart and fun, but I also wanted it to kick ass. Honestly, who lets a nineteen-year-old girl call the shots? My parents totally backed me; they let me take the meetings, listen to what people said, and, more importantly,

tell them what I thought my music should be.

When I made the video for "Kerosene," I wore the Junk Gypsies' "Mama Tried" tank top, and that kinda sealed the deal. We were partners in this journey. Part of the bond may be that the Gypsies are kids from a family business too. Their parents owned the first pizza shop in a really small town. They grew up around kitchens and hospitality, working hard, creating a space where people felt welcome, and knowing you don't get to check out whenever you want.

Their mom, like mine, is the cutest, toughest, funniest person. Our dads go hunting together. We're so interwoven, not only have the Sikeses come out to most of our shows over the years, but they've even been part of the boobs and tubes float. We normally don't let kids come—at least since Luke and I grew up—but Jolie's son and Amie's daughter have come with us several times.

When it was time for me to have my first real tour bus, man, who else would I get to design it? The Junk Gypsies, of course! We had, I think, one phone call, and they talked to Mom some, but I just let 'em go. After all, what kind of dreamer doesn't let another dreamer dream?

It turned out to be a pretty big deal. *Country Living* magazine put people on the bus for the delivery! They rolled out of College Station at 2 a.m. on a January day, and swung by to pick up my mom and dad. They made a really fun trip of it. They stopped in Memphis, stayed at the Peabody, went out to Graceland, Sun Studio, Beale Street—and eventually made their way to Nashville so I could see my first true custom coach.

The delivery was . . . well, I was almost speechless. I got on and walked through very slowly so I could take in every single teeny detail. They had "Twinkle, Twinkle Lucky Star," one of my most favorite Merle Haggard songs, over the bed. They had installed little plaques for towel hooks with Waylon, Willie, Merle, and Johnny in the back bathroom, so I could be near my heroes.

It was almost too much to take in. Up in the front, there was a gumball machine that said "Rainbow Stew," another great Merle Haggard song. We had black-and-white checked floors,

nailheads studding the metal counters, a zebra rug, a black velvet curtain between us and the driver, and crazy quilts on all the bunks.

Nobody ever had a bus like this, all rock-and-roll cowgirl. I loved it. When I put Wanda on the road, the Gypsies were the people I turned to.

One year for Mother's Day, they helped me redo one of my Airstreams as a surprise for Mom. Her favorite album of all time is Carole King's *Tapestry*. The Gypsies and I got together and plotted. (It's hard to keep a secret from Mom.) Or rather, I told them to go for it, then they did what they do. They got everyone Mom loves to give them a shirt, something they'd worn to an event or symbolizing a moment that each person knew she'd remember. They made the pillows and quilts out of the shirts, giving her bedroom a Bev Lambert *Tapestry* feeling. The cherry on top? They had a copy of the album framed on the wall.

When she walked in and saw it, she almost burst into tears. Shriek-joy-shock all at once. It was the best feeling to see her that happy. Just like our *Lion King* Christmas, Mom knew there were pieces of all of us that had been made into something so perfect for her.

When the Gypsies helped me do Mom's *Tapestry* Airstream, they had their HGTV show. So, even better, her gift became one of their episodes that season. Not only did Luke and I—and all the people who love her—get to give her this ridiculous surprise, but we also have video of how it came together *and* the look on her face when she saw it! Talk about high-quality home movies.

The bestest part about the Junk Gypsies: we're genuinely friends. When Amie and Jolie come out on the road, it's always fun. When the Texas Antiques Week in Round Top hits, their store is constant activity, with musicians on the porch, brunches, TV crews all over. Mom, the Ya-Yas, me, and my best friend April all tuck ourselves in at the Gypsies' Wander Inn. It's a little cluster of small barns they've turned into cool bunkhouses for like-minded travelers. Staying there puts us close to the action and brings the sisters (and their mom) into our world a little bit too. We *all* go, so two times a year, it's a guaranteed visit.

The Gypsies have always given us pretty much free run of the place, which is amazing. Even during Antiques Week, I can go pick up knickknacks; a top hat customized with pheasant feathers, flowers, and antique playing cards; stuff for the kitchen; cool books; or some kind of T-shirt with a great saying on it—and nobody even notices me. People are used to seeing me around there.

When the day starts to settle, Amie and Jolie come back to the house where we are staying. We build a fire, make some drinks, get some dips, and enjoy each other's company. We compare notes on which antique spots are rocking, what we're thinking we're gonna wear to Junk-o-Rama Prom, somebody we saw who really stood out—or just laugh about nothing.

The dogs run around. We break out the chicken salad or the charcuterie and just breathe in the open air. Maybe somebody breaks out a guitar and we sing a bunch of songs everybody loves. Just settle into the night. There's nothing like sharing a snack, catching up with old friends you don't get to see all the time, and hearing the gossip.

And if we're lucky, Amie, Jolie, or their mom, Janie, will bring over some of their catfish crabcakes. They took something fancy, looked around at what was easy to come by, and created an equally delicious version with something we'd all grown up on.

Taking something familiar and giving it an East Texas spin is about the coolest thing you can do. But with the Junk Gypsies, it's just another day at the office.

13

ROAD LIFE AND BACKSTAGE MAGIC

▼▼▼▼▼▼▼▼▼▼▼▼▼▼▼▼▼▼▼▼▼▼▼▼▼▼▼

Cocktails After the Show

When you're young, you look at those big, shiny tour buses—or even the older, pretty beat-up tour buses—and they seem like magic. You get on one, then it sweeps you away on this big gypsy adventure that Willie sings about as he spends his life "making music with your friends."

And that's true.

You're out there chasing the dream, playing with a band—*your* band. Then you escape into the night with a headful of notions, your people, and a whole lot of broken white lines on the highway. Some nights you can't believe the people who tell you how your song is part of their life. Some nights you can't believe how loud the crowd sang along. Some nights you're just hoping for a Waffle House up ahead, or a Taco Cabana where you can pull in and load up.

You know you can't count on much on the road. When it's not late-night, you can count on Cracker Barrel. They have a little bit of everything—

breakfast food, turnip greens, mac 'n' cheese—that tastes like home. When we were starting out, we used to look for the La Quinta Inns because they were *always* next to a Cracker Barrel.

There comes a point, though, whether it's out of self-defense or boredom during the hours you're not actually making music, when you start paying more attention to what you eat. You realize life is *not* about the next truck-stop cheeseburger or plate of greasy enchiladas. Delicious though they may be, eating that way catches up with you.

I live like a bachelor on the road. On my bus, my refrigerator usually looks like it's in a single guy's apartment. It's got a couple beers, some string cheese, and a few bottles of water. Sometimes I'll have eggs, because you can do a lot with a couple eggs—even make Mom's old-school deviled eggs.

Peanut butter and jelly remains the ultimate safety sandwich. Sometimes I bring homemade apple butter when we have time to make it in the slow cooker. If I don't have bread, I'll do it on crackers. It's to get you through. It's also what's easy.

I only eat one meal a day, and I don't eat dinner because I can't sing on a full stomach. I'm spoiled with catering. When they're making really good tuna salad, having the refrigerator stocked isn't as much of a priority. Our caterer Beth's the very best. Her tuna salad is a great snack. Whatever may be going on, I can eat a couple forkfuls or roll it up in some lettuce. It's an instant shot of good clean, lean protein.

Another part of keeping the refrigerator empty is the idea of "Who wants to eat alone?" Food for us is fun, friendship, and comfort. It's a reason to linger and enjoy talking to each other. So much happens on the road—all the stories, the glories, and the crashing disasters—and it's not real 'til we all come together and laugh about it. Granted, that happens after the show a lot of the time. Even if it's just over a little snack and a few cocktails, it's the coming together and the catching up that matters.

Once a weekend, when we have a lot of guests, we create the kind of night you've been reading about. A food truck setting up starts a vibe, and everybody falls into the more festive feelings. I usually choose Fridays for our parties. It's right in the middle of our run, and people who've worked all week can sense the vibe. Our group does too. Vibe is everything. We like vibe. Who doesn't?

Scotty Wray, one of my longtime musicians, a true, dyed-in-the-wool Texan, used to sometimes go into catering and look around, like, "What *is* this?" When the food was too bougie, he'd sigh. Now we actually have what we call the Scotty Wray Rule, which is taken from his very words: "Guys, can we just get something in a tub with gravy on it?"

In 2022, we lost Scotty, who'd been onstage with me for twenty years, which is almost my entire journey. A sweet soul, he believed in me like crazy; we weathered each other's triumphs and bad stuff for so many years. Beyond being a badass guitar player, he understood the roots of our raising.

Sometimes that matters more than you'd imagine. That Scotty Wray Rule kind of explains everything about the two sides of road food. Being out there, being gone, you want to eat right, but they call the other stuff "comfort food" for a reason.

Something really basic but well-made always wins. It makes people happy, keeps them feeling good and healthy, and allows us to come together—*and* it gives us a base when we decide to toss back a few cocktails.

In Texas, we take our drinking seriously. It's not about getting drunk or out of control—though that has happened—but more about having fun and the notion that a nice little buzz never hurt anybody. Hangovers aren't something we court, but if you know your limit and drink plenty of water, why not?

Plus, we're not driving.

YOU CAN'T LIVE LIKE THAT WHEN YOU HAVE A LOAD-IN TO HIT, DOORS opening at a specific time, and a curfew to finish by, but you can capture that spirit when the show's over. It's why I wanted Wanda so badly; not only is she a place for us to convene, but, when we're done playing, she also allows us the spirit of freedom that this highly scheduled life doesn't normally provide.

People don't think about what happens when the carnival is over, but it's a lot of waiting around to leave. Before the show, I can use Wanda for work things. If we have guests, I can make somebody a drink—and literally break the ice. It's a special way to be together with people from radio stations, local promoters or record store owners and employees, charities we partner with. Wanda and a cocktail take it from something orchestrated to "welcome to my little escape."

My mother was always entertaining people that way. It's in her blood, in Nonny's blood, in Lucy Miranda's blood, so I come by it honest.

After the show, out come the fruit plates, the vegetable plates, the dips. We go hard at either Death-by-iPod *now* Death-by-iPhone (where everyone tries to top each other's song), karaoke, or playing whatever instruments are around. There are some wonderful musicians out here, so getting a jam going is pretty easy. And this is when we get to play every kind of music imaginable. It's that spirit that drives some of the cocktails we've made up over the years.

When we opened Casa Rosa on Nashville's Lower Broadway, the idea was to bring some of that spirit into a place that was a little bit of my mom's cantina and a little bit of my road life, with a strong chaser of what's in my music. How do you distill the essence of all that into a cocktail? It's actually pretty easy.

When you sing about drinking and thinking, neon and jukeboxes, you've set yourself up for some pretty tasty adult beverages. You just have to figure out what it tastes like.

As a nod to my Texas truth and that hard-driving rock thing inside my music, where we lean in to ZZ Top, Stevie Ray Vaughan, maybe Charlie Sexton or the Fabulous Thunderbirds, there's the Locomotive. We're talking a slammingly spicy margarita that'll drive you to tears. The trick, beyond the spicy salt rim, is muddling pineapple chunks and fresh jalapeño slices. Whooo! You drink that with Heidi Crackers, and you're gonna have a good night.

The Bluebird is more my Tennessee-optimist side coming out. If you're going to be from Tennessee or Kentucky, you learn to love bourbon and whiskey; they're a slower burn than tequila, but they're smooth going down. We take a classic, Woodford Reserve bourbon, and add in muddled blueberries and mint; that puts it in a completely different place! Add a splash of lime juice for perk and a little simple syrup for sweetness. It tastes like my song "Bluebird" feels, and it even has a lemon wheel to reflect the lyrics.

Then there's a sort of fancy, girlie drink, because as much as I love a cold beer or a glass of wine, sometimes you want something a little sweeter, maybe even a little glamorous. The Miss Ohio, named for Gillian Welch's song about a beauty queen who wants to do right "but not right now," is everything a drink like this ought to be! It's the perfect pink, from mixing raspberry puree and raspberry- *and* berry-infused vodka with a bit of sour mix. Served in a martini or coupe glass for full effect, it's a "moment" for Instagram.

Be a little creative. You don't even need a shaker. Use what you got: mayonnaise jars if you wash them really well, or a jelly jar if you're just doing singles. Put in a little ice, whatever you're thinking, and shake it up! Next thing you know, you've got fancy cocktails without all the fancy equipment.

That's the beauty of this (extended) family: we celebrate everything. If you fall in with us, you will, too, because it's how we do.

We play the music too loud. We never know when to stop. We're not afraid of the morning after. It's why out on the road we always have the very best stories to tell—and the imagination to get into more tricks tomorrow.

MISS OHIO

MAKES 1 DRINK

1 ounce sour mix of your choice

½ ounce Raspberry Puree (recipe follows)

½ ounce raspberry vodka

1 ounce Berry-Infused Vodka (recipe follows)

Raspberry, for garnish

PLACE all the ingredients, except the garnish, in a shaker with ice. Shake vigorously. Strain into a sugar-rimmed coupe or martini glass. Garnish with a fresh berry.

TO make a sweeter cocktail, add ½ ounce simple syrup.

RASPBERRY PUREE

½ cup sugar

¼ cup water

1¼ cups raspberries

IN a saucepan, combine the sugar, water, and raspberries. Bring to slow rolling boil, stirring continuously, for about 5 minutes. Crush into a puree.

THE puree can be stored in an airtight container in the refrigerator for up to 5 days or in the freezer for 12 months.

BERRY-INFUSED VODKA

1 quart strawberries, stems removed

2 pints raspberries, lightly chopped

2 pints blueberries, lightly chopped

1 bottle vodka of choice

½ bottle berry vodka of choice

PUT the strawberries, raspberries, and blueberries into a large glass container and pour over the vodka. Let steep for 48 hours. Store at room temperature for 5 to 7 days.

LOCOMOTIVE

MAKES 1 DRINK

3 jalapeño slices

3 pineapple chunks, plus wedges for garnish

½ ounce simple syrup

1½ ounces silver tequila

1 tablespoon fresh lime juice

MUDDLE the jalapeño and pineapple with the simple syrup. Add to a shaker with ice, along with the tequila and lime juice. Shake vigorously. Pour into a margarita glass with a spicy salted rim. Garnish with a pineapple wedge.

BLUEBIRD

MAKES 1 DRINK

5 blueberries

2 fresh mint leaves

1 ounce simple syrup

2 ounces bourbon (I like Woodford Reserve)

2 tablespoons lime juice

Lemon wheel, for garnish

MUDDLE the blueberries and mint with the simple syrup. Add to a shaker with ice, along with the bourbon and lime juice. Shake vigorously. Pour into a collins glass with fresh ice. Garnish with a lemon wheel.

FAMILY, FRIENDS, FANS, AND ROAD CREWS

How Food Binds Us All

The way I grew up, we didn't always think about throwing a get-together; sometimes people just dropped by. They'd bring stuff. We'd share what we had. There was this attitude of "you can always make room at the table for one more." When they arrived with their slow cookers or casseroles, well, they were the friends who came bearing yummies.

Nobody loved friends and family like my parents or Nonny and Pop-Pop. And anyone who ever met Beverly Lambert landed inside one of the many layers of our family. It's why all my friends wanted to come by our house, even though we were so far out in the country; why Neicy and Rod and their kids would spend the weekend, not just come over for dinner or a Friday night porch-picking.

Even when we didn't have much, we didn't realize it, because there was plenty to go around. More than that, there was the adventure of pulling vegetables out of the dirt or taking tomatoes off the vine, playing with our chickens, and gathering up eggs.

Mom got us fed and brought us all together at the table. When I was in school, we had a class where the teacher asked how many of us sat down to dinner every night. My hand was the only hand that went up. I can't imagine my mother doing life at our house any other way. Same thing for Neicy, the Fischer sisters, the Junk Gypsies, and their families. There's something about what happens when everyone sits down together. You're grateful for what you have; you talk about what happened that day; you even talk about what you're hoping will happen tomorrow. There's no substitute for that. Why would you want one?

It's why when things get rough you'll find us in the first light of day, having our coffee and trying to sort out what needs to happen next. No matter how bad, when you're together and someone's making eggs or passing around Heidi's muffins, it doesn't feel so overwhelming or scary. They say there's strength in numbers, but you can take that to the power of four when you add in breakfast with the Ya-Yas.

Because our house was a constant open house—and my parents liked it that way—I grew up thinking, "Hi! What can we get you?" It was always about making people feel welcome and comfortable, and I'd like to think that as I grew up, I took some of that with me. Because from the boobs and tubes on the Guadalupe and my tenth birthday party, I saw how much fun you could help people have while you were having fun yourself.

When we were on the Lilith Fair, one of the few country artists among that caravan of girl gypsies, that idea of "come in" reached across all kinds of musical genres and created a space where we were all people who liked to play songs. It didn't matter what kind of music you made; if you were a person who loved songs, we couldn't wait to hear your story.

In a world of radio formats, that never gets to happen. You may be at the Grammys, where all the different kinds of music come together and are recognized, but you're rushing around among so many people all dealing with the realities of a live TV show. Out on Lilith, everybody liked the idea of kicking off their shoes and kicking back with a cocktail. We would compare stories about our different worlds, and suddenly a bunch of very famous people were transformed into a bunch of old friends telling stories.

That's what sharing food or drinks can do for you.

This carries over to my road life now. When Wanda's out, people know there's a place without judgment where you can sit around and talk about whatever's on your mind. It's a refuge and a chill-out spot. Because, as Nonny taught me, there's nothing a cheese ball and a few drinks can't do to smooth out the day.

Chasing around the world making music, I've met so many people. It's hard to remember every single person, but I hope if someone has come into our world, they went home feeling like they were special. To me, getting that opportunity to make someone a drink is a wonderful thing, not just because of how I was raised, but also because it gives me a chance to get to know them, to hear about their life and what makes them happy.

Songwriters are only as good as the people they meet and the stories they hear. Those tales keep your creativity inspired and your heart soft for what people are feeling. And sometimes you get to hear a crazy story or some adventure you wish you could've gone on. After all these years, it's still nice to hear how one of my songs impacted someone's life, gave them the courage to do something they might not have done otherwise, or showed them a window where all they saw before was a wall. It's fun, too, when you see or meet a group of women who're out having fun, being shameless about how much they're enjoying what's going on. My glass is raised to every single one of those females who get out there, rock as hard as they can, and don't care what people think.

When I'm home, it's amazing how some things remain the same. I'm always up for calling friends and throwing some Paw Paw Sauce on the chicken or sausage that's cooking on the grill. Use that as a reason to come together. I've learned over the years: it's the simplest things that leave the most room for the real heart-to-heart moments.

My husband, Brendan, discovered a bunch of new things through our tribe. So many of our customs confused him. He couldn't figure out why anyone would fry a perfectly good steak, or any steak for that matter. I'm not sure if we've got him on that country-fried steak with the cream gravy train yet, but boy, he sure can eat some Cajun food. So much so, it's almost like having a little bit of Neicy with me when he's making a roux for gumbo.

Food and celebrating are their own special language. It's how we share who we are with each other. It's how we make our love tangible. Wherever you are, whatever you do, know that. This book, if it does anything, should give you some tricks, some down-home dishes and flavors that'll make your tongue happy. Mostly, it should make you want to call up your own Ya-Yas, family, or friends.

In a world of social media perfection, people remember the laughter and how good things taste long after that fake and polished picture is forgotten. Sure, you want to make things pretty, and that's easier than you think. Don't be so worried about who does it better. Instead, think about who you're going to call to come over and help you chip that dip or fill up that potini glass.

As we all grow busier, with more texting and less talking, maybe this is an excuse to get together. Make up a big batch of Bluebirds, get some pimento cheese and Heidi Crackers, and just sit in your yard talking at the end of the day. Just like there's no substitute for someone's fingers on guitar strings, singing a song you love, there's no feeling like hearing your friends' voices or hugging someone's neck.

Here's to all your get-togethers, coffee klatches, morning-after brunches, and street-taco Tuesdays, as we call it. The Bitchin' Kitchen isn't a place after all. It's how the people you love make you feel when you're with them.

ACKNOWLEDGMENTS

There are so many people to thank for this project. I never thought I would be someone who'd write about home entertaining; yet, once we started, I realized my whole life was preparing for this very book.

Food has a way of bringing people together, creating comfort or an excuse to get together. It's something so ingrained in who I am, I don't even think about it. It just is. I've come to learn it's not always that way for others, so I am incredibly grateful that an idea to make a little church cookbook turned into what you hold in your hands.

I could write a whole other book of gratitude and appreciation, but for now, so many thank-yous to all of the following people.

My mother, who raised us in love and joy no matter how much or little we had. You instilled in me the importance of family, friendship, finding your way, being grateful for what you have—and knowing the importance of sharing those things to bring people together. You also instilled your outrageous sense of fun, of creating joy out of nothing, and of making every occasion a reason to celebrate. Your imagination, love of people, understanding of how to turn anything into a party and a party into a once-in-a-lifetime (until the next time) carnival of awesome literally colors how I face the day and try to make my world every bit as cool.

Heidi, Vicki, Mom, and Neicy, can y'all believe it? Our "fun little book idea" we dreamed about during 2020 is actually happening. What we thought was a little spiral-bound church cookbook turned out to be so much more. But even more than how this looks is the love you all put into it. It was so amazing to go back and listen to y'all tell some of these stories, to look at the pictures and relive all these memories we have made. I am so thankful to have women like you in my life. You have all taught me—individually and as a group—most of the things I know about life, how friends lift each other up, and the kitchen. I love you all so much.

Cheers to our pretty Bitchin' Kitchen!

Nonny, I love you and miss you every single day, but especially when I'm trying to re-create one of your signature dishes. I want to pick up the phone and call you, and just say, "How many cans of broth?" or "How the hell do you get those cookies to taste like that? I *know* it's not in the hands!" Thank you for all the after-school snacks, the rides in the Cadillac, the cheap bourbon and Cokes, and all the years of memories, as well as for sharing your joy and rhinestones with the world. I hope you are proud of this book. And maybe someday we will finally figure out the secret to the Nonny Cookies. Just know that I'll keep trying until I finally get there . . .

And to Pop-Pop, for putting up with us kids and for all those Thanksgiving turkeys you made. For sharing Nonny with us, and for all those shiny things you gave her as gifts that I treasure now and get to enjoy every time I look at them. I love you so much.

And Nonny's OG Ya-Yas: Pat, Peggy, Faye, Kay, and Joanne. I want to thank you ladies for showing us how to do it, all of it: life, friendship, cooking, drinking, smoking, gossip, and, most of all, love. You were so generous in what you shared with us, how you treated a little girl as one of your pack. You ladies were the absolute pros, and I'm so lucky I got to witness you all in action, as well as spend major birthdays, Halloweens, and countless afternoons watching your greatness in action!

Dad, there aren't enough words to thank you for teaching Luke and me about survival, in so many more ways than you could imagine. And for teaching us about character, which is more precious than diamonds, as well as the critical lessons of how to rescue cast iron, a dog, or a camper trailer and bring them all back to life. You taught us to "live off the land" when we were kids. In those years, I realized so much about myself and who I wanted to be through watching the way you embraced the world. Most importantly, thanks for teaching me those three chords. You were right: country songs only need three—and a whole lot of truth. Who knew where this would lead? But we did it! I love you so much.

Marion Kraft, thank you for believing in my art in every aspect, dimension, and possibility of the word. You have always encouraged me to grow and push the boundaries of what I think I am capable of. This book would not have happened if it weren't for you and Holly believing in it. I love you dearly, Mom Number 2. (Don't mess with Texas—or Germany!)

Holly Gleason, thank you for helping us tell our stories and for laughing and crying with all of us as we relived them together. You are a Ya-Ya now, whether you like it or not! But sincerely, thank you from the bottom of my heart for spending countless hours on this project, for caring about our sacred circle of love, and for pushing us to really tell our truths.

Joey Lee, I'll never forget the day you called my mama's house and she said, "Hold on, please." Then she whispered to me, "Nashville is calling . . . *finally!*" We both screamed when she hung up the phone with you. Then we flew all the way to Nashville on borrowed time and money. Once we met, we all knew right then that *this* was the beginning of our story together. And here we are twenty years later, still going and dreaming new dreams to make come true. Love you to death, Lynn.

Duane Clark, thank you for all these years of keeping me on track and believing in my art and my decisions without hesitation. You have always been such a fierce friend and protector to me. Even when it didn't make sense on paper, you understood and navigated this crazy journey. I am so thankful for our years working and dreaming together. And you are from Texas, so you know that means I love you extra!

Joel Shideler, you are the other piece of keeping this circus on the road. Thank you for being a true voice of reason in my world and for always having my back. People you can count on are precious.

Frank Liddell, you are a true song man. Thank you for all the hours we have spent either making music, listening to music, or drinking about music. You have taught me so much about art and my heroes. You are the person in my life who believes fully and makes sure to remind me that I always have another song to write. So, always because of you, I will keep on keeping on. Love you, my friend, for letting me color outside the lines, buck trends, and create music my way.

Margaret Riley King, thank you for believing in this project as something more than just a book about entertaining, and for letting Holly and me run off to Florida and get wild with words. I hope we made you proud, and that you know how much it means to me to bring all the love and community that food, drink, and songs have built in my world to the rest of the world.

Carrie Thornton, I know you are the George Strait of these kinds of books. You take all kinds of lives and turn them into road maps for other people to integrate into their world too. I hope this book speaks to lots of busy people who are looking for permission to come together, take off the pressure, and turn up the fun. Sometimes we *all* forget the power of a home-cooked dish shared with friends at a kitchen table; I appreciate you recognizing the value in that.

The Pistol Annies, Ang and Ash, my sisters and bandmates—thank y'all for sticking by my side through all the life we have lived together. I am so blessed to be a part of this band we made up and this sisterhood that runs deep. We get to write our stories together as a united force, and nothing can replace that collective feeling of us as one! We gotta make all these snacks on our next writing excursion, because I finally got those "bitches" to write the recipes down! Love you both.

The Junk Gypsies—thank you, freewheeling sisters, for your never-ending mix/match/fluff/flame/vintage imagination and inspiration. Your style, your grace, your family, and your passion are so intoxicating. I'm lucky to call you "framily," the friends who became part of our family. I'm so honored to have y'all be part of this book! Can't wait 'til Round Top and Junk-o-Rama Prom. Love y'all dearly and appreciate how you help me invent my world.

All my songwriter pals, you know who you are. Thanks for taking these journeys with me. You let me be who I am in the room, no matter what that looks like at the time. You encourage me to tell my truth, open my heart, and share what's on my mind. Together we find songs that give other people their truths too. What a community to be part of.

Luke, you are the true cook and brains of the family. Thank you, little brother, for having my back and believing in this crazy dream with me for our whole lives. You listened to the first songs I ever wrote, and you pretended they weren't shitty. Talk about love!

I am so very proud of who you are and all the things you teach me just by being you. Proud to be your big sister and your biggest fan.

And finally . . .

My husband, Brendan. Thank you for loving me the way you do and for jumping into this crazy country music world we love and live in with no fear. You are pure joy—and you spread it everywhere you go.

We both know you are the one who does the cooking, yet somehow I have a book about food here—but let's let that be our little secret. Hahaha. Thanks for showing me what true Italian food should taste like and for always making me dinner and being my best friend. I love you. Now it's *your* turn for a cookbook, babe!

(Oh, and thanks for joining Holly and me on all our long workdays in Palm Beach, for bringing us frosé, and for reminding us that the stories would still be there tomorrow but maybe you and I should go play in the ocean a little bit too.)

HOLLY GLEASON WOULD LIKE TO THANK . . .

Miranda Lambert for being as committed to getting it right on the page as she is about what happens in the song or on the record. Marion Kraft for bringing me to this incredible circle of love. Bev Lambert, Heidi, Vicki, and Neicy—as they will now always be known to me—for not just their incredible memories of the details but also for believing in a young girl's dream in a way that allowed their friendships to inspire and inform her music.

All of you have no idea how powerful the love and friendship you exude actually is. Just being around you fabulous women is dizzying, thrilling, at times overwhelming, and ultimately a potent reminder that no one gets through life alone. For trusting me with all of your triumphs, tragedies, and journeys, bless you.

Laurel School for Girls, which taught a dyslexic young woman that it's possible to blaze an impossible trail—just remember the details and try to capture the stories as you go. Jeremy Tepper and The Outlaw Country Cruise for being an exemplary place for the push to the finish, especially Steve Earle, Emmylou Harris, Carlene Carter, Rodney Crowell, Lucinda Williams, Asleep at the Wheel, Rosie Flores, and Mojo Nixon for inspiration that matches Miranda's passion and study breaks that never broke my writing groove.

Green's Pharmacy, the Country Inn on Military Trail near Hypoluxo, and Howley's Diner for refuge; Charlie Pickett and Laurel Burns for being stronger than dyslexia; and Kathie "BFK" Orrico, C. Orrico, and Classic Bookshop on South County for loving everything about "my secret project" from the very beginning. Closers Rob Simbeck and Wendy Pearl for good sense, sanity, and the bottom line; Jamie Callender for use of "the house of Eddie Rabbitt's monkey."

Wherever you are, whatever you dream, use this book to set yourself free—and use snacks to create memories of your own. It's never as hard as it seems, but taking a few pages from this book, you might be amazed at how delicious having fun can be.

CREDITS

Recipe testing by
Michelle Cudd, President, RHL Inc.

Food styling by
Tami Hardeman, food stylist
Abby Gaskins, food styling assistant
Matthew Mosshart, food styling assistant

Principal photography by
Emily Dorio

Additional photography by
Jamie Wright
Spencer Peeples

Family photos courtesy of
Miranda Lambert/Lambert Family

Prop styling by
Lily Noel

INDEX

Note: Page references in *italics* indicate photographs.

ABOUT THE AUTHOR

MIRANDA LAMBERT is from East Texas. One of the most celebrated artists in country music, she is the most awarded in Academy of Country Music history, taking home thirty-eight Academy of Country Music Awards, including Entertainer of the Year. She has won three Grammys and fourteen Country Music Association Awards, including seven Female Vocalist of the Year Awards. She married former New York City police officer Brendan McLoughlin in 2019, and spends time on the road, in Texas, and on her farm outside Nashville. Lambert is a successful businesswoman, who spearheaded Casa Rosa, the only female celebrity–helmed restaurant on Nashville's iconic Lower Broadway; Idyllwind, her rock-and-roll cowgirl–inspired boot and clothing line; Wanda June, her Miranda-centric home goods line; her family's The Pink Pistol, home to her Red 55 Winery wines; and MuttNation Foundation, her dog rescue charity.

mirandalambert.com
🄾 mirandalambert
🄳 mirandalambert

HOLLY GLEASON created *Woman Walk the Line: How the Women in Country Music Changed Our Lives,* winner of the 2018 Belmont Book Award, and received the 2019 CMA Media Achievement Award. She's written for *Rolling Stone,* the *New York Times,* the *Los Angeles Times, SPIN, Interview, Playboy, Oxford American,* the Library of Congress National Registry of Recordings, NPR, *Variety,* and *Musician.*

DEYST.

Page 271 serves as an extension of the copyright page.

HarperCollins books may be purchased for educational, business, or sales promotional use. For information, please email the Special Markets Department at SPsales@harpercollins.com.

FIRST EDITION

Designed by Renata De Oliveira

Library of Congress Cataloging-in-Publication Data has been applied for.

ISBN 978-0-06-308778-1

23 24 25 26 27 WOR 10 9 8 7 6 5 4 3 2 1